To my LONGTIME
FRIEND,

BILL O'SHAUGHNESSY —

ALL MY BEST,

Marlin

RADIO

RADIO

MY LOVE, MY PASSION

MARLIN R. TAYLOR

MASCOT BOOKS

www.mascotbooks.com

Radio...My Love, My Passion

For more information, please contact:
Mascot Books
620 Herndon Parkway #320
Herndon, VA 20170
info@mascotbooks.com

Library of Congress Control Number: 2017918629

CPSIA Code: PBANG0118A
ISBN-13: 978-1-68401-592-4

Printed in the United States

CONTENTS

Please visit **www.marlintaylor.com**, where you'll find more stories, photos, and color versions of several of the photos that appear in this book.

ACKNOWLEDGMENTS

I am most appreciative and grateful to the special people who have played a role in bringing this autobiography to fruition.

First and foremost, Alicia, my wife and partner for forty-two years, who has been supportive and loving throughout all of our years together. And, in my writing of this memoir, she's provided encouragement during what proved to be a rather long journey, along with valuable insights and proofreading and even improved this book's title.

I thank our friend Jennifer Owens for her professional editing services.

Our good friend, Fritz Haberman, who devoted many hours to reading every word, who made suggestions and asked questions, which led to my clarifying the verbiage in numerous places.

I cannot forget Ken and Sylvia Smith, who provided never-ending encouragement over these last years as I labored to complete this, the story of my professional life.

To Walter Powers and Greg Katkowski, key members of

the BBC team, for helping to fill in blanks in my memory related to dates, incidents, songs, and stations as we took our programming to music lovers in more and more cities across the nation.

Three very skilled individuals who worked in the programming production area of XM Radio/Sirius XM and helped shape the "tone" of our presentation were, on the 40s Channel/Savoy Express, Jim McBean and Matt Wolfe—who took London's Big Ben and "taught" it to play XM Radio's five-note signature—and, on enLighten, Paul Sacilowski, who knew instinctively the exact right piece of music to use to enhance the spoken message of our station identifiers.

There's Erik Logan Toppenberg, XM's Senior VP of Programming during the years prior to the merger of the two companies, who took action to provide me with the support I deserved and recognized the value and benefit of providing enLighten with a channel on XM's satellite service.

And there's my longtime friend, Dr. Bruce Mims, Professor of Mass Media at Southeast Missouri State University, who has provided counseling as I've worked my way through this entire process leading to the final step of publishing.

And Jerry Lee... and our great partnership which resulted in the successful launch and building of WDVR in Philadelphia, which propelled us down the paths of achievement we each have been privileged to enjoy in these many years since. As a marketer and promoter, Jerry's in a class by himself.

I must say a heartfelt "thank you" to Michelle and Kristin and their team at Mascot Books for their diligent attention to all the details involved from the time we committed to going forward with this project right through to when we had that first copy of this finished book in hand.

Finally, I know there are others whom I could or should recognize by name but sadly don't remember, or if I did, I'd likely hurt others because I overlooked or failed to mention them. However, to all who have helped me and helped create and deliver the audience-satisfying programming product we brought to the airwaves over these many years, I say a most sincere "thank you!"

INTRODUCTION

This book is primarily the telling of one man's love affair with radio broadcasting, which began in earnest seventy years ago, and my extended journey within that industry. This is only unique in that it has involved many twists and turns along the route, but there was always the element of programming for a radio audience involved.

I've chosen to call it *Radio... My Love, My Passion*, yet it could just as easily be titled simply, *The Adventures of Marlin*. By the time you get to the end—if you get that far without falling asleep—I think you'll understand why the latter title could be fitting.

My passion for radio had its beginnings when a young boy became enraptured with the multitude of sounds that emanated from a small plastic box which had a couple of knobs and a funny-looking dial on its front. Every time you turned one of those knobs, the sounds changed—a love affair that's still very much alive after all these years.

Encouraged by folks after sharing about events that took

place over the years in the industry, I realized I had to get this all down in some form—for me and anyone else who'd be interested. So, with this encouragement, I committed to sharing my story, not so much because I've lived a life that many will necessarily find interesting. Rather, because if I can plant some seeds that will inspire or help someone who's been contemplating entering the field of communication or journalism, this effort will have been worthwhile.

While today so much of what is called "media" is tied to pictures or the visual aspect via television and the Internet, we might forget that in 1946, it was sound as delivered through the air by the magic of radio. This created what is called "theater of the mind," where the action and the scene were painted in your own mind, and which can still be effective when done well.

As I write this, it's been sixty years since I was offered my first paying job in the radio industry. I state it this way to be completely honest, as I have not been employed in at least one broadcast-related position continuously for all of those sixty years—the total is closer to fifty years. There were two notable gaps, one coming during a portion of the thirty-eight months I spent in the military, and the other during a fair part of the 1990s. Still, during those periods, even if not physically involved, my heart and mind were still totally connected to the radio industry and its goings-on... never did my love for it waiver at any time. I still wonder how many copies of *Broadcasting* magazine were being mailed to Thule Air Force Base in Greenland during the years of 1959 and 1960—I know there was at least one.

As much as anything, you might call this an historical document, as so much has changed—especially in technology—from when I got that first job in 1956. The way we did things back then is considered almost laughable today. At that time the term "computer" was barely known and the transistor was a recent invention. Without those two developments, we'd still be living in what could be called the dark ages when it came to broadcasting and so many other areas of life. Today, we give little thought to how these devices enhance our lives. Furthermore, two terms that today's kids can relate to before they're even old enough to go to school, "Internet" and "social media," were still more than forty years down the road. In addition, who would have ever thought that as the calendar turned over to a new century, something called the Satellite Digital Audio Radio Service would be launched. Or that one of the two companies licensed to operate by the U.S. Government would eventually be named XM Satellite Radio (based in Washington, DC), and that in the year I became eligible to collect Social Security, I would be hired to be one of its many program directors.

What is written here draws mostly from the depths of my memory bank, assisted by archival material (some of which you'll see at points throughout the book) I've managed to preserve through many moves over the years. In addition, I have spent quite a bit of time researching for confirmation of any actual dates or other facts stated, to address any question of accuracy and to satisfy my own curiosity. Considering that it covers more than half a century, this book can be considered a mini-history of radio broadcasting as seen through and interpreted by one individual who's lived through more than two-thirds of the life of radio broadcasting itself, which will just be 100 years old in 2020. Where possible, I've included photos, although I have never been a taker of pictures, especially as related to my work.

Originally, my thought was to dwell primarily on the successes and exciting aspects of my journey and gloss over the "downs." However, since this is likely the only book I'll ever write, I think it only fair and proper to include the warts as well, since many occurred because of rapid emotional decisions rather than stepping back and reviewing an action based on common sense and good business judgment. Related to this...there is not a day that goes by that I'm not thankful for the hand I've been dealt in this life. It has had its ups and downs, but they have kept me humble and remembering my roots.

I must be honest and say that I did not have any set goals when I was young. All I knew was (1) I needed to make a living, and (2) I loved everything about radio! However, once I became intrigued with what I could hear hour after hour, day after day, my mind became focused on how I might get on the other side of that box, so that I could play a role in creating those magical sounds that filled my ears.

As I share this journey with you through the following pages, there are events and actions that, while maybe not described as such, will involve what can be defined as one or more of the following: passion, intuition, dedication, pioneering, creativity, innovation, and even what might be considered guerrilla-like tactics. While radio is quite different from what it was when I was so fortunate to be offered that first position in 1956, even from what it was twenty or thirty years ago, I believe there are still opportunities for creative people who are willing to put forth the effort.

Along the way, I've included a number of side stories related to broadcasting that provide a little humor or an interest-ing insight into the world of radio. At the same time, hopeful-ly, in some way, parts of my story will prove educational and/or inspirational for readers who are looking to enter the realm known today as "the media" or are seeking a way to move to the next level in their chosen field. And, it's my hope that my story will prove interesting to the casual reader, especially those who have an interest in radio, its history and some of its inner workings.

Whenever I mention to someone that I spent much of my life in broadcasting, they immediately want to know my name, thinking that possibly I was a personality they heard on their radio at some point. I quickly tell them that I was not a star or celebrity, nor did I seek to be. I worked behind the scenes to create programming that they may have listened to. Yet I do feel honored to have had the opportunity to bring joy and comfort to the hearts of millions across the land for multiple decades—stretching over more than half a century—and to have left the legacy of three of the most popular formats that continue to be heard today on SiriusXM Satellite Radio.

I recently read that when legendary musician José Feliciano was asked how he'd like to be remembered, he responded, "as a man who tried to bring peace through his music!" Facts are facts; I have no musical talents for performing or even to read music. Yet, I seem to have a gift for listening with the ears of the masses. All I wanted to do in life was choose and program music and create relevant programming that would add joy to the lives of others, too many of whom, for one reason or anoth-er, lead what can be called humdrum lives.

At the same time, I believe that having the insight to recognize this is the real key to the success I've enjoyed. In an article printed in the June 21, 1971, issue of *Broadcasting* magazine, I'm quoted as follows: "I don't think broadcasters have ever given the general public enough credit for being really conscious of what they are listening to, or really having the ability to hear." That's why my battle cry for decades—too often falling on deaf ears of the parties who most needed to hear it—is, "the listener is number one!" We in radio are the merchant with a product to sell; the listener is the customer. Yet, to this day, so many decision-makers in broadcasting take the approach of creating and delivering what they think the listener *should* like and accept because they themselves like it, or take shortcuts in creating the programming product to save a few dollars, assuming that the listener won't know the difference. Because this approach has become so widespread, the radio industry as a whole is suffering. There's an old adage, "you've made your own bed, now lie in it."

Also, I believe that my continued passion for what I do after all these years comes from an inner desire to always be looking for something unique, such as a special or unusual piece of music or bit of information, or even a forty-one-hour documentary which you'll read about in Chapter 13, that will capture one's attention, thereby giving that person satisfaction from listening.

It's been an interesting ride. Why I was granted the wonderful experiences I've had along the way, including my share of ups and downs (with a number of the downs being of my own making) is still something I question at times. I never claimed to be a genius, even particularly smart; it just happened that I was gifted in a particular way that tied in perfectly with my passion and that I was fortunate enough to have the opportunity to establish a career in this area of love and expertise.

How did I achieve the success I've had for the better part of these past fifty-plus years? What demonstrated talents, experience, and training did I possess? I could not sing, play an instrument, or read music. I did not go to college—there were no dollars for that and, frankly, no real desire on my part. Radio was my love, my passion. I never even thought about college as a place to learn or gain the necessary skills for a career in broadcast communications. My education in radio programming began when I got that first radio at age ten!

During my nearly two decades with the Bonneville organization (which you'll read about beginning in Chapter 8), my employment contracts described what I possessed as "a peculiar talent." I have always felt privileged and honored to have been blessed by the Creator with the ears and discernment of the masses, to design and assemble radio programming that has been meaningful to millions over many years.

My hope is that in reading this, you'll sense that as I have lived my life, no matter what the circumstance encountered along the way, I've maintained a positive attitude and sense of optimism about what could or might be achieved—that is the only route to success that I know.

CHAPTER 1
My Early Years

"The two most important days in your life are the day you are born and the day you find out why."

MARK TWAIN

When did my love affair with radio actually begin? I'm not quite sure. However, I can without a doubt say it definitely became serious after my mother gifted me, her only child, with a radio of my own in 1946. During the years of 1942 through 1945, virtually all manufacturing facilities were devoted to supporting the massive war effort. But following the end of World War II, companies were returning to producing products for the consumer market.

What motivated my mother to purchase the radio for me? I'm not really sure, yet there was at least one incident that may have set the stage. One afternoon in the early 1940s as I was walking up our country road in the rural area north of Philadelphia, Pennsylvania, I spied a pile of phonograph recordings sitting in front of a neighbor's house, awaiting the trash man. I can't say that I'd ever seen a recording prior to that, but instinctively I knew what they were and knew I had to have them. I couldn't run home fast enough to get my wagon and return to collect this group of 78-rpm discs.

Since we didn't have a record player of any sort in the house, I had to contain my excitement until mother had enough money to find and buy me an inexpensive one. The one she found had a turntable which ran on electricity, but the sound came out of a mechanical diaphragm speaker that sat above the needle on the pickup arm. I quickly learned that these needles would break easily, and replacements weren't easy to come by when you lived out in the country. I also learned that you could cut off and use the tip of a safety pin as a substitute, but that surely shortened the life of the recordings.

I estimate that this phonograph record experience occurred when I was no more than seven or eight, and the player was likely manufactured prior to the country's factories going into full war production in early 1942. I imagine the record player was not new, possibly given to her by a friend or someone she worked with after she told them of my phonograph record experience.

This may well be what led my mother to sense that I had a love of music and that having a radio, instead of allowing me to listen to just a few recordings, would enable me to experience a whole new world of music and drama and comedy and information. I was ecstatic and I could not wait to eat it up! This is when the advanced education that would serve me for life really began.

From the minute I received the radio, my ear was glued to

it during every available moment. My first memory of listening to a radio broadcast came when I was six. It was on Sunday, December 7, 1941. Other family members and I were gathered around our Atwater Kent console radio in the parlor of our home in Bucks County, Pennsylvania, listening to news reports of the Japanese bombing of the naval base at Pearl Harbor, Hawaii. How my family learned of what was happening half-way around the world, I do not know. I do not remember the radio being turned on with great regularity. We did not have a telephone, so possibly one of our neighbors up the hill had come down and told us. Or, it may have already been evening and the radio had been turned on to listen to the Jack Benny program or another Sunday night show.

Also, I can't say how much of what we were hearing and the impact it would have on our country registered with me. After all, I had just turned six and was only in the first grade. Yet, from the reaction of family members, I realized that a calamitous event had taken place. In hindsight, I wonder how many Americans recognized the name "Pearl Harbor," and how many really knew where the Hawaiian Islands were located. However, this would soon change.

If the name Atwater Kent is new to you, let me fill you in. First, there is Arthur Atwater Kent, the man. By his college years, he had developed a reputation as an inventor. Sensing an opportunity, by 1923 he had founded the Atwater Kent Manufacturing Company and quickly became the largest maker of radio receivers in the United States. Produced in a plant in Philadelphia, the Atwater Kent radios were of high quality and in great demand. The company reached its peak in 1929, manufacturing nearly one million radio sets. With the coming of the Great Depression, the demand for Atwater Kent's expensive receivers declined. So, rather than cheapen the quality of his product, Mr. Kent shut down his radio manufacturing plant in 1936. Hence the disappearance of the Atwater Kent name.

Do I remember hearing news reports along the way during the WWII years that followed? Not really. However, I can vividly remember the demands that we lived with on the "home front" during the war years. Because we were within so many miles of the Atlantic Ocean, there had to be heavy curtains over the windows at night if lights were to be turned on; also, electrical tape was put over the top half of vehicle headlights to lessen visibility from the air at night. There were "air raid" alert signs posted everywhere and volunteer wardens, who were charged with enforcing the laws and letting us know if there was a drill or actual warning declared. Plus, there were the ever-present ration stamps, required in order to purchase gasoline and critical food items. The man who would officially become my stepfather after the war was drafted into the Navy, and my Uncle Raymond was called to serve in the Army.

My next true radio memory occurred on April 12, 1945. When I arrived home from school that afternoon, I walked into the house and found my mother ironing with the radio on, playing sad-sounding music. I sensed something was wrong, and then

World War Two ration book and a sheet of stamps, recently uncovered in the archives of the van Wagenen branch of my family.

Mother said, "President Roosevelt died today." In that era, radio was how we heard and learned about important events.

Several months later, as the war came to an end, I became the proud owner of a Philco Transitone table radio, which sold for the mighty sum of $19.40...quite a bit of money for a single mother to afford in those days. The price of that radio might well, as noted earlier, be considered the cost of my college tuition because, more than simply enjoying the programming being broadcast, I analyzed how different shows were produced and the elements that went into making them so appealing.

One of my favorite musical personalities was Martin Block, who was the original host of the Make-Believe Ballroom on WNEW in New York, later moving to WABC in the Big Apple. I also enjoyed listening to a wide variety of programs, including afternoon serials like Tom Mix and Sky King. Then there was the 950 Club on WPEN in Philadelphia with Joe Grady and Ed Hurst. Disk jockeys like Block and the duo of Grady and Hurst were popular because they always had stories and funny bits to keep listeners interested.

Philco radio

These were just a few of my primary choices, as I regularly scanned the dial on this AM-only radio to see what the other area stations were programming, in addition to seeing how many distant stations I could pick up. One of those after dark was WCKY at 1530 out of Cincinnati, which played country music, although the mail order offers seemed to occupy more of the hour than did the music. Then there were really distant stations like XERF, a Mexican-licensed station from Del Rio, Texas, which I could hear some nights after our local Pennsylvania daytime station on 1570 signed off. At 1540 AM, there were nights I'd pick up KXEL, a 50,000-watt station in Waterloo, Iowa–likely the smallest community in the nation to have a clear-channel station licensed to it. Other nights, when atmospheric conditions were different, ZNS from Nassau in the Bahamas could be heard on 1540.

Later on, Al "Jazzbo" Collins became a nighttime fixture on WNEW, and his unique approach caught my fancy. His show originated from the "Purple Grotto" and he was kept company by his Purple Tasmanian Owl.

At times, I'd listen to the evening network shows by Fred Allen, Jack Benny and sometimes Eddie Cantor and Jimmy Durante, plus the *Aldrich Family* and everybody's favorite high school teacher, *Our Miss Brooks*.

When I became old enough to discover and really become enamored with radio, it was still in its golden age, since television did not make an impact on radio until the beginning of the 1950s, as good chunks of the country were still awaiting their first

School photo of yours truly, age twelve

TV station. A lot of smaller metropolitan areas would get only one station at the outset, with many other communities having to wait for the arrival of stations in the UHF band in the mid 50s–this is what initially brought forth the concept of cable TV.

While Philadelphia, the metropolitan area where I grew up, got its first station in the late 1930s as an experimental facility owned by the Philco Corporation, the second did not arrive until late 1947 and the third in 1948. When NBC launched *The Milton Berle Show* in the fall of 1948, only a very small percentage of American homes had a set; our house did not get one until the early 50s. As I think back, my real interest in getting a TV set lay in the fact that WPTZ in Philadelphia had begun a morning show with my zany old friend Ernie Kovacs and I ached to see it.

Those with sets in those early years quickly learned that, during most hours of the day, most channels aired the same program: television's most popular transmission, the test pattern. When's the last time you saw a test pattern?

Initially, outside of a few cities in the northeastern United States, most viewers had to watch kinescope recordings of the network shows, as the telephone company's video-capable network was not completed coast-to-coast until late 1951. If you ever saw a kinescope, you remember how poor the quality was, as it was actually a film recording recorded off a television screen, and the development of videotape was still a few years away.

I also liked baseball during those years, listening to By Saam and Bill Campbell broadcast the Athletics and Phillies games from Shibe Park (later Connie Mack Stadium) in Philadelphia, where both teams played. I even put together a play radio station control board using a cigar box and pieces from a Tinker

Toy set so I could "broadcast" the games on my station.

It wasn't long after receiving my radio that I discovered the one and only Ernie Kovacs, who in the late 1940s was being heard on WTTM, a radio station in his hometown of Trenton, New Jersey. WTTM always had a broadcast booth at the annual New Jersey State Fair, and I became a great fan of Ernie's when, in the fall of 1949, he allegedly was on the air live around the clock from that booth for the full eight days of the fair, Sunday through Sunday, without sleeping. During the many hours of the schedule which were live and local, Ernie's was the only announcer voice heard. However, WTTM was an NBC affiliate, which allowed him breaks during daytime and evening network shows. I say "allegedly," as engineer friends reported that he took catnaps during the network time; however, he needed to be awake for station announcements be-tween programs. Broadcasts that originated from outside the studios, including the dance band remotes that were late-night net-work staples into the early 1950s, have al-ways held a particular fascination for me, right up to this day.

Ernie Kovacs.
Courtesy KYW-TV/WPTZ
Philadelphia

At the same time, I've always had a love of wacky, slapstick comedic routines—the ultimate in creativity—whether musical numbers or just plain stunts and stories. I'm not sure which came first; my encountering Ernie Kovacs on radio (where he wasn't nearly as funny as his later routines on television were, as they benefited from the visual aspect) or my mother and stepfather taking me to a performance by Spike Jones and his City Slickers at the War Memorial Auditorium in Trenton. The latter made such an impact on me, I can still visualize it today, nearly seventy years later. I think this interest has played a role in how I've looked at and addressed certain things in my programming over the years— but more on that later.

I enjoyed my high school years, where one major activity of mine was playing records for dancing in the gym at lunch time plus the occasional evening dances during the year. The other was showing the educational films which the teachers used extensively in their classrooms in those days. By tenth grade, I'd become the primary person handling the projection of these films, which consumed two or three class periods on most days of the year. This required me to transport and set up the projector, speaker, and screen multiple times a day. I enjoyed this and I've been known to remark that I "majored in movie projection" in high school.

By the time I was in my teens I was helping at our local fire company summer carnival. To get ready for the event, I would assist Uncle Raymond in running electrical lines and wiring the booths with lights. Then, I'd set up a battery-operated public address system on one of the fire trucks, play music, and promote the carnival as the truck was driven around the community. During my high school years, since by then we lived near the center of our village north of Philadelphia, I was borrowing several big horn speakers and tying them to the roof of my parents' house so that I could serenade the community with Christmas music during the holiday season. Apparently, most who heard it must have enjoyed it...if anyone did complain to the police, I never knew about it.

Speaking of police, I was called out of bed at 2:00 a.m. one morning in August of 1955, after the Delaware River and its tributaries in eastern Pennsylvania overflowed their banks, sending torrents of water downstream due to two back-to-back hurricanes hitting the region to the north. Two of the river bridges north of Trenton were swept away, with hundreds of homes in Bucks County being inundated with flood waters, causing fear of an outbreak of tetanus infections. My mission: get the battery-powered portable public address system mounted on my car and get on the road, going through areas near the flooding, urging residents to immediately go to a community center and get their tetanus shots. I did this for the better part of the next forty-eight hours.

By the 1950s, as mentioned earlier, I was paying less attention to the entertainment itself and began thinking more about what was behind what I was hearing... the mechanics, the creative aspects, and trying to understand how it was pieced together and why—what did one do to connect with listeners and keep them coming back for more? What funny bit would Ernie Kovacs come up with next, or how would Martin Block introduce his next recording?

The key was finding ways of building an emotional and personal connection with the individual listener so that he or she became yours, as long as you kept reliably delivering what they were anticipating and didn't take advantage of them. I have always believed that the only way a competitor could take a customer (i.e., a listener) away from you is if they were to provide a product or service vastly better than yours, meaning that you were not keeping up the quality of your product, such as providing fresh and new content, instead allowing it to deteriorate and become stale.

When I first became recognized for having the skill to create radio programming that the masses truly loved and wanted to listen to, I was asked repeatedly where I went to college to learn how to do it. I still maintain that much of what I have instinctively done over these past six decades is not something that can be learned in a classroom. If it could be, then the much-admired communications schools have failed by not teaching it! It's my feeling that when it comes to possessing an intuitive sense, you are either born with it or develops in your early years, likely conveyed genetically.

My mother, who never lived more than a few miles from the farm where she was born into a "dirt poor" family in 1913, always marveled at how her son was able to eventually follow his dreams and become successful in radio in the big cities of Philadelphia, Boston, and New York. When my parents married in the 1930s, my father was a milkman, delivering bottles house to house, and was a small-town musician with his own combo, playing clubs in the Trenton, New Jersey area. (At some point, I was told that he was an extremely talented musician and a great trumpeter, possessing skills fairly equal to those of such top names as Harry James.)

My mother always loved music and sang in her high school chorus, yet she demonstrated no particular creative skills beyond that. I must assume that from these two people I inherited the innate senses for music and the programming of it, which became my ticket to my half-century-long career in radio.

I grew up not really knowing my father. My parents divorced not long after I was born, and I'd see him no more than a half-dozen times in the succeeding sixty years, with half of those visits coming in the last few years of his life. Also, I did not have many playmates in my early years, as we lived out in the country and had few neighbors. Despite these circumstances, I was raised well by not only my mother but by my Nana, my mother's mother, Aunt Irene and my stepfather, who came into my life by the time I was of school age. It was he who taught me the rules of being a man; to have a work ethic—such as helping to grow and harvest large quantities of vegetables and being on one end of a two-man crosscut saw—and to deliver on your promises. He also retrained me early on to call my mother "Mother," not "Mommy" or whatever other child-like name I had been calling her. I didn't have the benefit of grandfatherly love, as both grandfathers had died before I was old enough to know them.

My wife Alicia and I recently drove through the area where my family lived during my early years and saw the first house that I can actually remember living in. We resided there from when I was three or four through the end of WWII in 1945—about seven years later. During the early years, there were three generations and two families under that roof: my mother and me, my Nana and step-grandfather, my uncle and aunt and their two oldest children, my cousins Nancy and Connie. This is also the place where I got my first real taste of radio, sitting with family members on that Sunday in 1941, listening to reports of the bombing of Pearl Harbor—a day and incident in our nation's history we must never allow to be forgotten.

From the outside, the house doesn't look too different today than I remember it; in fact, nor does the area in general, except that a few years after we moved a few miles away, the eastern end of the Pennsylvania Turnpike was built, which cut through barely two hundred feet from the house.

A vivid memory about the building of this highway was that it took out a beautiful stone mini-mansion that sat in its path, built just a few years earlier by renowned artist Arthur Meltzer and his wife, Paulette van Roekens Meltzer, both teachers at the Moore Institute of Art in Philadelphia. (Some time before we moved, Paulette Meltzer did a portrait of a young version of me in pastel—it was not given to my family and there's no catalog of her art, so we have no idea if it still exists somewhere.) Much of the construction of their home—the beautiful wood flooring was held in place by wooden pegs, not nails—had been done by Arthur Meltzer himself. The Turnpike folks allowed the Meltzers to remove as much of the house as they could haul away, and Arthur proceeded to build a new home at another location.

In addition to my fascination with radio, throughout my life I've had an attraction to trains. Primarily, I enjoy watching and reading about them, which likely can be traced to my proximity to the main line of the Reading Railroad, which was just a couple of hundred feet across a field. The Reading ran from Philadelphia to Trenton and up through New Jersey, connecting with the Central Railroad of New Jersey. This allowed its express passenger trains to run from Philadelphia to Jersey City, New Jersey, including its premier express, the *Crusader*, the image of which I'd copy fifty-plus years later to create the logo for XM Radio's 1940s/Swing Era channel.

My intense interest in radio and radio broadcasting played out through constant listening to many different stations and programs and always analyzing what I sensed did or did not connect with the listener. Despite this, a lot of time passed before I took action to involve myself in the behind-the-microphone side of broadcasting. I was nearly twenty before I got up the courage to visit a station (I was definitely introverted in relating to others until I had gotten to know them).

I had seen two live TV productions previously, both while still in high school: I had seen a teen studio show at WPTZ in downtown Philadelphia, and during a class trip to New York City, I had managed to get tickets for my buddy, Bob Rogers, and myself to a network half-hour situation comedy, which aired live from an old theater in midtown Manhattan. I don't remember the name of the show, but I think it was on CBS; it would have been 1952 or early 1953, at least a couple of years prior to the introduction of videotape.

And that pretty much brings us up to when I was offered my first job in radio, marking my official entry into the broadcast industry. What follows includes a bit of radio industry historical information, my memories of the industry and those who were part of it over the years, and my own experiences working in it for the better part of the past sixty years. In addition, I've included the philosophical approaches used to achieve the successes that I've been blessed with during this time period that has seen radio go through tremendous changes.

CHAPTER 2
The Beginning of a Career

One Saturday afternoon sometime in mid-1955, I finally drove the dozen or so miles to Trenton, New Jersey, to find 416 Bellevue Avenue. This was the address for the studios of WTNJ, a small daytime-only AM radio station—which meant it had to sign off at sunset. What I found was a stately old stone house in a residential part of town among many similar homes dating to the earlier part of the 20th century. I don't even remember there being a sign on the building.

I tried the front door and it was unlocked, so I wandered in and followed the sound of the music coming forth, leading me to the smallest room in the building. It was the control room, where I found the Saturday afternoon DJ, Ray McFadden, whom I had been listening to on the way there.

While I had never seen or met him, I had listened to Ray a couple of years earlier when he was the morning announcer on

Philadelphia's smallest station, another AM daytimer, WTEL. Ray's shtick there was that he called himself, "Ray Fred, the man with the two first names." Then, at 9:30, the station had a half-hour program of light classical melodies which they called the Music Hall. Since this was a more formal presentation, his name became Raymond Fredericks!

Even though I'd not been in many radio stations to this point, I'd seen enough pictures of "modern" broadcast equipment to recognize I'd walked into a radio broadcast museum, as virtually everything I saw dated to the 1930s. Prior to the end of World War II, outside the major cities there were not many radio stations in operation, and of course, all stations were on the AM band except for a handful of (mostly experimental) FM stations. More than three-quarters of all the stations operating in the U.S. in 1955 had begun broadcasting during or after 1947. Hence, the equipment manufacturers had, by the time they again began building station control and transmitting components, come up with new designs incorporating the newest technologies. Many of these technologies were born of developments made for the military during the war. Even so, by the end of the 1930s, the Radio Corporation of America (RCA) and Gates Radio Company had begun producing studio control consoles that had a contemporary look about them and greater functionality.

Ray greeted me warmly and, learning of my intense interest in radio, welcomed me in. As time went by, this became my Saturday afternoon routine and Ray was happy to have the company and have me answer the telephone when listeners called with requests.

One Saturday, after several months had passed, Ray said that he and Al Liebert, who was the morning show host, had signed a contract to do a live Saturday afternoon show from a car dealer showroom on U. S. Route One across the river in Pennsylvania. Since doing the broadcast would require more equipment than this antiquated station possessed, and knowing that I had a fair amount of audio gear, they offered me the job of being the show's engineer... if I brought along the missing components, which proved not to be a problem. My first paying job in radio! This began in early 1956 and continued until early summer, when the show moved poolside at a nearby swim club for the summer months.

A quick technical inventory: The station had a Western Electric remote broadcast mixer that could handle four inputs plus connect to the telephone circuit to the studio. It also had numerous 1930s-era Western Electric microphones, none of which had likely been used in many years, along with a turntable mounted on a bulky wooden box that didn't necessarily play on-speed. It was my good fortune that I had met an audio-visual dealer in the area who had two RCA Model 74 microphones that he was interested in trading for a 16-mm sound film projector that I owned.

These mikes, which were first marketed in 1935, were head-and-shoulders above the Western Electric ones, being of a new design known as ribbon velocity; that is,

RCA Mike

they had a corrugated foil ribbon that sat between two large magnets and captured the sound waves. This man didn't consider the mikes to be worth much, as they did not function. Taking them apart, I quickly realized the ribbons had been damaged. So, I took a trip across the river to Camden, New Jersey, to get replacement ribbons from RCA, then carefully installed them, and voila, they performed like new. I also owned an RCA 45-rpm changer into which I'd installed a better-quality pickup cartridge that would serve just fine, as we played only those little discs with the big holes.

Now the challenge would be to connect these to the Western Electric unit from the 1930s, which had input sockets for large, twist-lock plugs common to heavy industrial 220-volt power cables. My microphones were equipped with the 3-prong microphone plug known as an XLR that's been the audio industry standard since the late 1940s. I went to an electrical supply store to purchase several of the plugs—metal shelled and measuring over an inch in diameter—to match to the remote mixer sockets, so that I could assemble adapter cables.

Since it was designed for live microphones, the Western Electric mixer did not have any setup for cueing records, as do all more modern broadcast mixer/control consoles. So, how would I cue the next recording to be ready and keep the program flowing? My solution was to wear headphones and turn up the volume on the record player channel just enough to hear and do it gently while the guys talked. Everything came together and worked well and we had a great eight-month run. Of course, all of this activity was part-time weekend activity. Through these years, following high school graduation, my full-time "day job" was in the technical side of manufacturing specialized industrial electronic equipment.

By this time, the Sunday morning operator/announcer had departed, and I was hired to fill that position. Some months later, a transmitter attendant was needed for Sunday afternoons, so I took over that job as well. (As

FCC License

WTNJ was a daytime-only station with a non-directional signal–only one tower–a first-class licensed engineer was not required to man the transmitter; my third-class Federal Communications Commission (FCC) license was sufficient for the task.) At noon, I'd leave the studio and quickly drive the five miles to the little building and tower in the middle of a large field, where the mid-1930s-era transmitter with its open grillwork would heat the building in cold weather, and the building doors and windows would be opened to "air condition" the transmitter and engineer in warm weather.

I've always been fascinated by this station's history. WTNJ was Trenton's first radio station, going on the air in the early 1920s as WOAX. It was owned by one Franklyn J. Wolff under the corporate name of WOAX, Inc., assuming the WTNJ call letters sometime in the mid-1930s. It would be the city's only station for twenty years. Even then, it was not a full-time station. As was the case in several cities across the country, two or three AM stations would share the same frequency, even though not all of the stations were in the same community. In the state of

New Jersey, three stations were licensed to operate on the same frequency (1280 kilohertz and later 1310 kilohertz): WCAM in Camden, WCAP (later WJLK) in Asbury Park, and WTNJ, each broadcasting with 500 watts of power. The schedule had both WCAM and WJLK operating simultaneously for several hours and then signing off for WTNJ to have its turn.

By the late 1940s, many more stations had begun broadcasting, and the owners of the Camden and Asbury Park stations desired to operate full time in order to be competitive. Hence, they petitioned the FCC for relief from the share-time commitment and resolve the matter of overlapping signals. This was accomplished in 1949 by moving WTNJ over one channel to 1300, reducing its power to 250 watts and licensing it to operate during daylight hours only. The other two stations would remain on 1310 and be authorized to broadcast full time but have their transmitting power also reduced to 250 watts in order to minimize interference with WTNJ.

The large old stone home that housed the studios and offices was only partially utilized by this point in the station's life, as the station's format was primarily music with disc jockeys.

From documentation I can find, the station had a complete re-build in 1938 and '39, moving into this building and constructing a permanent transmitting facility across the Delaware River in Pennsylvania... all equipped with the latest mid-1930s Western Electric studio and transmitting equipment. Not much information from earlier times is to be found, except that it seems the station may have had a rather transient life until permanently settling into 416 Bellevue Avenue under WOAX, Inc., ownership until finally being sold in 1959. After the ownership change, it got new studio equipment, changed to a Top 40 format, took on new call letters (WAAT) and became "Watt Hot Jet-Stream Radio 13."

Nearly half of the building's main floor was consumed by a large studio that barely ever had a human set foot in it, although I'm sure that in earlier times it was the home to many live broadcasts by large and small musical groups alike. The small control room, where I found Ray McFadden, was originally meant to house only the control console for this big studio, two turntables for playing an occasional 78- or 33⅓-rpm transcription disc, and an engineer. (By the time I arrived on the scene, they'd managed to squeeze in two more turntables that played LPs and 45s.)

To the left of the control room was an auxiliary studio that measured about 20 by 20 feet. The rest of the ground floor consisted of the reception area and a tiny announce booth that was used by the newscaster and the Sunday morning foreign language show hosts. After I offered to help, chief engineer Nick Dalessandro built new cabinetry and installed wiring for moving the operational facility into the 20-by-20 room, with our transferring the old broadcast equipment to the new location over a Saturday night; there were no funds for purchasing any new or additional components. The DJs were finally able to breathe and not suffer pangs of claustrophobia.

To have a broadcast facility totally outdated in just sixteen years might seem to be quite rapid. However, between the mid- to late-1930s and the end of World War II, barely ten years later, especially for smaller stations, radio went through a great transformation. Gone were most musical ensembles and live drama involving multiple individuals; in their place were single individuals reading news and commercials or hosts introducing recordings, no longer needing big studios. And, outside of larger stations in larger cities, the announcer or DJ on duty worked—as Ray McFadden did—from the control room and ran the controls himself.

There were several large rooms on the second floor (originally bedrooms prior to station days), which housed offices for the general manager and business manager plus the record library, such as it was. The remaining room, other than the building's one bathroom, which was three or four times as large as the box the DJ's were working in the first time I visited the building, was one where the door was always closed, but not locked. Upon opening the door, my first reaction was that it was a giant dumpster, as there were no shelves or furniture of any sort and nothing was in boxes. Yet, upon closer examination, the heap of paper that dominated much of this 12-by-10-foot room, contained a great deal of interesting radio-related information covering a great span of years.

I relate this latter bit of information simply because, for a young man whose love affair with all things radio was unquenchable, it was like finding a treasure trove of interesting pieces of information, including scripts for producing radio shows that dated back many years. One finding was a script for a thirty-minute presentation on George Frideric Handel's writing of the famed oratorio, the *Messiah*.

It was December 1957 and time for me to dive into my first radio production. For the musical portions of the production, I took my trusty tape recorder over to the Trinity Cathedral in Trenton on a Monday evening to record the Trenton Community Chorus, a 150-voice ensemble (this was where I would first meet my beloved Alicia, who eventually became my wife). The program's narrator was Ron Poleo, a weekend host at the station.

From what I was told, the station at the time was owned by an elderly brother and sister who lived in New York City. It's likely it was Franklyn Wolfe, whose name continued to show up from time to time through the 1940s as president or general manager, and his sister or Franklyn's heirs. Their business affairs were being handled by one Erling C. Olsen, who was a New York investment advisor and author of meditational volumes that still can be found on Amazon. My first contact with Mr. Olsen, in name only, was when I took on the Sunday morning studio duties, when we aired a half-hour evangelistic message of some ilk by him just prior to the Hungarian Hour.

Through my time at the station in the mid-1950s, the advertising sales staff consisted of the three DJs. Otherwise, there was a receptionist/traffic manager (the person who handled the advertising contracts and scheduled the commercials for broadcast), a business manager/billing clerk and the general manager, as well as the engineers who manned the transmitter and a couple of weekend announcers. Speaking of the engineers, I'm reminded that the studio had only one reel-to-reel tape deck. This was used only for recording pre-produced commercials, which had to be recorded when the station was not broadcasting, as there were no other facilities. While the engineers were at the transmitter, they were very much involved in programming operations, as they had two tape decks from which they inserted into the programming all of the non-live commercials.

While I would not consider the programming anything exceptional, at this time in the station's history it benefited from having a rapidly expanding market with great population growth, thanks to the building of Levittown, Pennsylvania, and a couple of other large housing projects in lower Bucks County. These were situated immediately across the Delaware River from Trenton and the actual location of the WTNJ transmitter. Along with the growing population came a multitude of new businesses, all needing name exposure and customers.

I want to share a couple of memories relating to the two air personalities I worked with at WTNJ. First, of course, was Ray McFadden. A new, aggressive car dealership, McCafferty Ford, had just opened, and Ray had signed them for advertising on the station. Not long afterward, they began advertising during the late movie on one of the Philadelphia TV stations. In those days, many TV commercials were still delivered live, and Ray was selected to be their TV sales voice. This immediately led Ray to proclaim himself to be the "Fabulous Ray McFadden."

Al Leibert, who was also the station's program director, was a very different sort; he was focused on the creativity he could bring to the airwaves. Today, radio morning shows are all about multiple personalities, character voices, and the like. In the 1950s, this was virtually unheard of, yet Al was doing it. I would marvel at his creative use of multiple voices and sounds in his show, extracting them from the numerous transcription discs. The discs arrived weekly, and contained fifteen-minute and half-hour dramatic and other shows for the station to broadcast during their "public service" time. He was a man ahead of his time in this area, especially considering how difficult it was to pull off given the antiquated and limited equipment we had at WTNJ—a single reel-to-reel tape deck and a couple of turntables. By late fall of 1956, Al and his creative talents were off to WGBS, a large AM station in the much larger market of Miami, Florida.

In short, commercial radio broadcasting was very different during its earliest years than it was following the war. The changes came with even greater acceleration as time progressed through the fifties and into the sixties. The arrival of FM and the continued building of new AM stations and the splintering of formats, as well as the vast technical improvements available to station operators made it much easier to have one-person operations while handling many more elements. Then, what a change there was in the forty-plus years from the late 1950s, when music was played directly from 45s and LPs, to the early 2000s, when an entire radio station could be run from a computer screen, with all of the music and pre-recorded commercials living on its hard drive.

I didn't stay with the Sunday afternoon transmitter watch for more than a few months. I continued the Sunday morning studio work, where I played public service programs mixed with a couple of live foreign language shows, until I was drafted into the United States Army in June of 1958.

So, my budding radio career would be put on hold; at the time, I didn't know for how long. However, it would turn out to be not much more than a year.

CHAPTER 3

Thirty-Eight Months with Uncle Sam

ince Uncle Sam's invitation to join the United States Army didn't offer any alternatives, I was soon headed to Fort Jackson, South Carolina.

Of course, not many radio-related opportunities presented themselves during basic training. However, I volunteered to be a "fireman," meaning that every fourth day I was responsible for the coal-burning stoves that heated the water for showers in each of the four barracks and, if needed, provided heat for the building. That turned out not to be necessary, as the daytime temperature averaged 104 degrees during much of our eight weeks there. (The alternative to being a fireman—which required about two hours of work spread over twelve to fourteen hours—was KP duty in the mess hall, which demanded laborious work over something like sixteen hours.)

At the end of basic training, I received orders to report

to Fort Knox, Kentucky, to be trained for tank operating duties, which likely would have included a year or so of being stationed in Korea. In this case, though, these orders did come with an option: commit to an extra year of military service and you'd be granted an assignment more of your choosing. After a little praying, I felt this offer was worth the gamble. After all, I didn't have any great opportunity or event awaiting me at the end of the two years.

You may remember Nike missiles of the Cold War era and their many locations around major metropolitan areas, especially along the two coasts. Well, my next stop was the southern New England region of Nike sites. Throughout my remaining thirty-six months of active military service, God was taking care of me. When we arrived at the headquarters in New Britain, Connecticut, while most of the guys were shipped off to the individual launch and control sites to be what we called "missile polishers," it so happened that this very day the unit was in need of a new clerk in personnel to handle finance records. Again, I volunteered, and once I proved I could add and subtract, I had the job.

We're in the Army now!

While there were no radio opportunities for me in Connecticut either, I did spend some time hanging out with the night announcer/DJ at WHAY, an AM station in New Britain. That's where I encountered a radio personality named George "Hound Dog" Lorenz ("the Hound is around!"), who was syndicating a nightly show out of Buffalo, New York that aired on

WHAY. (The owners of WHAY would add an FM sister a few years later and, come the late 1970s, my programming would be heard on it.)

One of the highlights of this time in Connecticut was having the opportunity to go to the Bushnell Memorial Auditorium in Hartford and hear Annunzio Paolo *Mantovani*, better known simply as Mantovani, conducting a symphony-sized orchestra performing his legendary arrangements, including his major hit, "Charmaine."

My stay in central Connecticut proved to be shorter than anticipated. About the time I was getting comfortable there, the spring of 1959 brought orders that I was needed up above the Arctic Circle at Thule (pronounced "Too-Lee") Air Force Base, Greenland, where the Nike missile 7th Artillery Battalion was on duty, protecting our base and radar installations should a Russian missile suddenly come flying over the North Pole. Again, I would be a personnel clerk.

Thule is nearly 700 miles north of the Arctic Circle and less than a thousand miles from the North Pole. It is situated on the northwestern edge of Greenland on Baffin Bay, which separates it from the northern islands of Canada. From another perspective, it lies 2,500 miles nearly straight north from New York City. In spite of its name, the large center portion of Greenland was at the time—even though it today reportedly

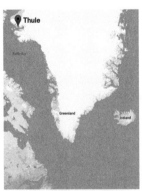

The location of Thule Air Force Base in relation to northern Canada and the United States—courtesy of Google Maps

continues to melt and shrink—covered by an ice cap. Around the edges, at least in the northern portions, the earth is frozen as well, what's called permafrost—meaning the soil is permanently frozen.

Arriving in mid-May, we were midway through the four-month period of total daylight. Darkness would not begin to return until August, initially for a very short span. During this time, temperatures were usually above freezing, with the warmest day of the summer of 1959 peaking at 68 degrees. Not long after this, however, the temperatures began dropping and soon came the first snowfall. We would see snow coming out of the sky over no more than the next two or three months, and there was never more than an inch or so on the ground. By the time we'd seen the last bit of sunshine on a day in early December and entered the winter night, we had seen the last snow falling; from then on, it simply blew around until temperatures rose from their low of minus thirty to above freezing, and then it melted. Daylight began to return in mid-February.

Upon arrival, I quickly learned that the base had two radio stations, but only one was operating at the moment due to a burned-out transformer in the 1,000-watt transmitter. This was May; by September the transmitter repairs had been completed. The next question was what to do with the second station, as no one seemed to remember what it had aired previously. At the same time, it was discovered that someone had presented the stations with a large collection of RCA Victor LPs, the bulk of which contained classical music and Broadway shows. While continuing my day duties, I volunteered to operate the second station a few hours each evening, programming from this LP library.

By the way, this station carried the call letters KBIC (Kripes, But It's Cold) and was on 1210 AM; the main station at 1425 AM was KOLD! I would later dub the station "the warm voice of the cold North!"

After working about thirteen hours a day between the two jobs for three months, I was exhausted and ready for a break, so hitched a ride on a C-124 "Flying Boxcar," a cargo plane returning to Dover Air Force Base in Delaware, for a ten-day leave at home in Pennsylvania. Upon my return to Thule, it was Christmastime and my Commanding Officer finally agreed to allow me to be the Army's representative at the stations as my full-time job. As I was the only known person on the base that had any previous radio station experience, I was assigned to handle the evening shift on KOLD, which gave me the opportunity to do a four-hour disk jockey show, which I did until my year's assignment ended in late April of 1960.

Somewhere along the way, I've got to acknowledge that I am a rebel with an entrepreneurial spirit. It has served me well over the years and has been beneficial to my career, even though there were times when the outcome was not positive. My first decision regarding the DJ show was to name it Cousin Ray and the Platter Parade, akin to the way they did things in commercial radio at the time. This name was in contrast to most others, who identified themselves as "Airman Jones" or "Sergeant Schwartz." (In my earlier years, I used my middle name when on the air, as I felt "Marlin" wasn't a particularly good radio name.)

While my fifty-plus years in broadcasting was primarily devoted to programming, this was my one and only stint as a DJ. Anyone who heard me could tell you, this was not my forte. A side story related to this, though, was the fact that the Armed Forces Radio & Television Service provided their stations with sixteen-inch discs called "transcription recordings," which contained the songs that someone at headquarters felt appropriate for stations to play. However, with the rock-and-roll era in full swing by 1959, AFRTS was not providing nearly all of the new records that the young troops wanted to hear. Soon after I took over the evening shift, I heard from two or three guys who regularly received mailings from home of new releases on 45-rpm records. They would bring them down to the station, and I would go through the discs and copy to tape any that I felt right about playing.

This not only provided me with an expanded library to draw from, it also served a second purpose. Several times a year, Thule had wind storms (like hurricanes but without any appreciable precipitation) they called "phases," numbered One through Four in intensity. The station's studios were in a four-room frame building that sat on wooden blocks—one of the flimsiest structures on the base. So by the time a storm got to phase Three, we could not play phonograph recordings: the needle would not stay in the groove as the building bounced. So, with a good collection of songs on tape, we were able to keep the music flowing!

As a side note regarding my programming of the evening DJ show, I mostly played current and recent pop hits, as that's what the troops craved. However, one of my most favorite pieces of music to this day is "The Battle Hymn of the Republic." Somehow, it was providential that I could play this selection and yet stay within the format criteria! It so happened that the recording of it by the Mormon Tabernacle Choir would find its way onto the *Billboard* magazine Top 100 chart and climb into the top twenty positions during October and November of 1959, just weeks prior to my taking over the show.

Remember, this was still several years before satellite communications and, if there were telephone lines, they were primarily for actual telephone calls for military and other important purposes. We had both voiced newscasts available from AFRTS and teletype news from the Associated Press via Strategic Air Command headquarters in Nebraska, but both had to be picked up via shortwave radio signals, both of which were very unreliable up there in the North. So, if we got some news by either of these means, we felt lucky.

You may ask, "what filled the remaining hours of the day on KOLD?" Primarily edited versions of shows from the U. S. commercial radio networks along with shows produced at AFRTS headquarters, all arriving via these same 16-inch transcription discs. These played at the same 33-1/3 rpms as LPs, except that the grooves were larger and required a different pickup stylus.

I did not consider my year in Thule a hardship, as I was doing what I loved for much of the year. While it was cold there and rather isolated, this was not what I'd call a barren outpost. At that time, there were about 5,000 military personnel stationed there along with another 5,000 or so civilian construction workers who were building out the infrastructure of the base and constructing the huge Ballistic Missile Early Warning System radar facility, located up on the hill above the base itself. Out of this number, as far as I know, only three were females—all serving as nurses at the base hospital. Also, around the bend of Baffin Bay was a small Danish village with several hundred residents; at the time, Greenland was a county within the nation of Denmark, although Greenland is several times larger than the entire Danish country itself.

Part of the base infrastructure that was still being built were the water and sewer lines connecting to all of the buildings. Because of the low temperatures, the pipelines had to be wrapped in insulation and electrical heating lines, so the construction process was slow. Among the last buildings to be hooked up were the four Army barracks, which was logical, considering that we were on an Air Force base. Without the pipeline connections, water and sewer trucks had to be relied upon. Again, being Army buildings, these barracks received the poorest service. So, if the sewage tank was full or the water tank empty in the building, no showers or other water-related functions were possible. Why do I tell you this? Once I became the night DJ, we entered into a little military bartering (in commercial radio in the U. S., this is known as "payola" and is strictly illegal). I called the dispatcher responsible for water and sewer trucks and found what his favorite songs were. From then on, as long as my barracks received good service, his favorite songs were heard regularly; otherwise, they would happen to fall off the playlist.

Likewise, this routine served us radio station workers well when it came to getting transportation to and from the stations' building via the base taxi service, which normally was reserved for officers and other higher-ranking personnel. Plus, while the only non-work-related chore I could not get out of was KP (kitchen police), the mess hall chief always made sure I had the easiest job; usually as dining hall attendant. In addition, he would get me out in time to get down to the station for my 8 p.m. show. During much of the half-year I was full time at the stations, we worked a six-hour shift seven days a week, as we were short on staff.

There were two other sources of entertainment available on the base: the movie theater, which showed six different films a week, plus KOLD Television, which operated several hours each evening. Being that this was before the days of videotape and satellite delivery, it relied on kinescope recordings of network TV shows, which arrived almost daily except when flights weren't able to land due to wind conditions. You see, the runway had been carved out of the side of the large hill that rose almost from water's edge for several hundred feet. The winds were frequently too strong for planes to land and take off safely. When this occurred, station personnel would resort to showing one of two films that were permanently in their library. I only remember one of the titles, *Seven Brides for Seven Brothers*, which was broadcast an average of at least once a week.

Neither of my trips north to Thule, both when initially being sent there and on the return from my December leave, was routine. We'd take off from McGuire Air Force Base in central New Jersey on our Military Air Transport Service (MATS) C-118 and get up past Labrador, Canada, and perhaps even up to southern Greenland, when the pilot would come on the intercom and say, "Well, conditions are presently too poor for landing at Thule and don't look like they'll improve today, so we'll turn back and land at so-and-so." I remember spending a night, possibly two, at Goose Bay, Labrador, as well as at an air base near St. John's, Newfoundland, and at Sondrestrom Air Base in southern Greenland. At that time, it was operated by the U. S. Air Force and was also a refueling stop for SAS commercial flights from Scandinavia to central and western North American cities. Today, it has a new name and is owned by the government of Greenland.

For my next assignment, I had applied for and was granted permission to attend the Army Information School's eight-week journalism program. At the time, the School was at a small Army post, Fort Slocum, located on David's Island, just off of New Rochelle, New York, in Long Island Sound. There was no bridge connecting the island to the mainland, only a ferry for crossing the body of water that wasn't much wider than a few lengths of the small ferry boat. Adjacent to the ferry dock was the Glen Island Casino ballroom, made famous prior to World War II by radio broadcasts of the Glenn Miller Orchestra's many performances there.

As I remember, the principal item we were taught was the writing of press releases and short newspaper articles. What little there was related to radio, I had already learned from experience even before my year in Thule.

Next, I headed south to Fort George G. Meade, located between Baltimore and Washington, D.C., where I'd spend the remaining thirteen months of my service time. My first stop was the office of the post's newspaper, where we were expected to find and write about interesting happenings and people. I quickly learned this was not my calling, as this was a military installation where not very much of note occurred with any regularity. As such, most stories were about happenings that weren't at all noteworthy, and I have never been good at writing fiction. The newspaper would have been much more interesting to the average reader (if anyone read it at all) if we'd written about our experiences and what went on in places like Thule, Greenland.

The sergeant in charge of the department also produced a weekly thirty-minute show about happenings at Fort Meade which aired on WBAL-AM in Baltimore, so I spent time helping produce the program.

An anecdote related to this activity involved the department's two large reel-to-reel tape recorders. I'm not sure of their origins, as they had no brand name on them. Apparently, the military had ordered a quantity of them at significant cost savings rather than purchasing from Ampex, the major maker of professional recorders at the time. However, the units had a major flaw: when you pushed the "stop" button, the brakes would apply instantly and, in most cases, break the tape. I tried adjusting the brakes, but there were only two results: the instant-stop-break-the-tape outcome or no appreciable stopping control, which generally caused the tape to start flying off the reels as they slowed. Eventually, I devised a solution that worked: putting some 3-in-1 oil on the felt brake pads so they wouldn't grab.

As it was evident that this was not where I belonged, I was transferred to the publicity department of the Second Army Recruiting District, headquartered there at Fort Meade, to work with Sergeant Patrick in the radio department. The mission there was to produce weekly fifteen-minute "public service" shows that stations located in communities all over the Mid-Atlantic states (Virginia, West Virginia and parts of Pennsylvania and Maryland) would air, primarily on Sunday mornings, to fulfill their promises to the Federal Communications Commission of so many hours of public service time per week. Distribution at that time was via seven-inch reels of tape, each one containing two shows. (Fortunately, this operation had none of the tape recorders that the post information office was stuck with.)

My small amount of knowledge in electronics served me well here, as I quickly discovered that equipment repairs and modifications were needed to make the facility more functional. Other than producing a weekly show featuring country music, which was the favored music in much of the area that we served and in which the sergeant had no interest, it was my duty to duplicate the tapes and package them for shipment. It was also fortunate that the Army Language School's Training Department was located on the post, as it had an excellent high-speed tape duplication facility we were able to use.

I had been a subscriber and reader of *Broadcasting* magazine since early in my Trenton days and always checked the section that listed new stations being granted by the FCC, as well as changes in station ownership. By this point in my Army tour of duty, I'd come to understand the importance of "intelligence." In the military, it relates to gaining knowledge of and about the "enemy." In the business world, this would be defined as learning everything you can about your competition or, in the case of seeking employment, an organization that you'd like to become part of before any action is taken or direct contact is made. In other words, if you don't read the right sections of trade publications, you are likely to miss some real opportunities or miss gaining some valuable knowledge about an industry or organization.

In all of my years in broadcasting, I can remember responding to classified ads on only two occasions that resulted in my becoming involved, one for employment and one for the purchase of a radio station—neither of which proved to be a smart move on my part. Both situations are described later in this book. However, this inquisitiveness, this desire for having the facts about anything that might be transpiring within my sphere of interest, has been a key contributor to my being where I am today.

In this case, as you are about to read, this action would prove to be a godsend. My great love of broadcasting, especially radio, was exciting. However, my resume was pretty thin when it came to qualifying for a position of any real sort in the industry. My experience involved being a remote broadcast engineer and part-time control board operator, but I was not a qualified engineer capable of repairing a transmitter if it broke down. I was an announcer and disk jockey on an armed forces radio station that served 10,000 people on a remote base in the frozen North. I had no experience or interest in advertising sales. I had no demonstrated skills in programming or managing air talent. So, I saw little opportunity except hopefully to get in on the ground floor of a new operation where I could prove and develop the skills that I was confident I possessed.

In early 1961, I had just a few months left on my enlistment and was about to get married as well. Then, a listing appeared in *Broadcasting* magazine for a new FM station being granted for the Bethesda, Maryland, suburb of Washington, D.C., with the call letters of WHFS. Included were the name and address of one of the two gentlemen who had secured the construction permit. As Bethesda was only a thirty-minute drive from Fort Meade, I was quickly in my car and on the way to find the home of Robert J. Carpenter.

CHAPTER 4

My First Full-Time Position in Commercial Radio

"*O ne Saturday shortly after Broadcasting Magazine announced the grant of our CP (construction permit, as granted by the Federal Communications Commission, allowing the applicant to build a broadcast station to the specifications as stated in its written application), a soldier appeared at my front door, looking for a job. It was Marlin Taylor, then assigned to Fort Meade, Maryland, but he had nearly completed his enlistment.*"

Those are the words of WHFS co-founder Bob Carpenter, with whom I continued to be in contact until his passing in early 2016, as he documented the early history of this FM station licensed to and located in Bethesda, Maryland, on the fiftieth anniversary of the station's launch on November 12, 1961, as published in *Broadcasters' Desktop Resource.*

My first knocking on Bob's door occurred sometime early in 1961. After we chatted for some time, he saw enough potential in me that a meeting with his partner Bill Tynan was arranged. Together, they concluded that I had sufficient understanding of the overall operation of a radio station and appeared to be responsible enough that they could entrust their station license in the day-to-day hands of this guy who likely displayed more enthusiasm and passion than experience. And, even though I didn't have a very good voice for radio, I did know how to talk. Plus, on the monetary side, my demands fit their budget.

Bob goes on to say, "*Marlin became our only full-time employee for most of our ownership. It is impossible to over-estimate the jack-of-all-trades effort he put into the station. We had a broad format running from 'Hi-Fi'* (including what was known as 'ping pong' stereo) *music, through light and more serious Classical to Jazz, plus Broadway cast albums and full operas on weekends. Marlin was able to pick music for any category.*"

By the time they agreed to employ me when I was discharged from the Army in August of 1961, they had secured a 20-foot by 20-foot space adjacent to the caretaker's apartment on the lower level of an office building, along with an agreement for installing a tower on the building's roof to hold the FM transmitting antenna. We had three rooms: a control room, a transmitter room, and a larger room that served as office and general work space.

Beyond retaining his full-time job with the National Bureau of Standards (now the National Institute of Science & Technology), Bob was busy constructing components of the broadcast technical facility, as he was building a fair amount of it from scratch, including the control console and portions of the transmitting system. As I commented at his memorial service, Bob began his endeavor with not much more than a pile of junk radio equipment and a box of electronic parts.

There aren't too many things which were more crude-looking than our transmitter, the cabinet of which was a welded frame of angle iron with metal plates bolted to it. According to Bob Carpenter, the unit was originally built for Major Edwin H. Armstrong. Armstrong was the inventor of frequency modulation (FM) radio, who apparently used it for testing purposes at various locations and had provided it to one Everett Dillard so that he could construct an FM station in Washington, D.C. That station became, and is still known as, WASH. By 1960, this transmitter was no longer being used, so Bill Tynan was able to acquire it from Mr. Dillard along with an RCA FM exciter, the portion of the transmitting system where the programming audio is inserted and which sets the exact frequency on which the station is licensed to transmit. It all came at a price, as Bill says, "we could afford."

For the technically inclined, I'll note that all broadcast transmitting equipment must be approved by the Federal Communications Commission. When a manufacturer of such equipment produces a new model of any component, their first step is to gain approval for it from the FCC, so when a station acquires it, no further authorization is needed. In the WHFS situation, the only part of our system that had FCC approval other than the antenna was the old RCA exciter, and it was designed for the original FM band, located between 42 and 50 megahertz. Today, of course, all FM stations operate between 88 and 108 Megahertz, where FM was relocated in 1945. (Just think, today the FM band is jammed full of stations, and others would like to get on; whereas the original space was less than half the size of the present band.)

First, the actual transmitting part of the transmitter was built for test purposes in the 1930s, and the RCA exciter couldn't deliver a signal within the new FM band, so Bob had to construct a component to raise its output frequency to 102.3 megahertz. All of this, along with the stereo-generating component, which I'll discuss in a moment, would require approval from the technical department of the FCC.

How were we to get this accomplished within a reasonable amount of time? Fortunately, both Bob and Bill were electronic engineers who had long lived in the greater Washington, D.C. area and were well connected to the engineering community of the nation's capital. Within that group as well was one Robert E. Lee, an engineer who happened to also be a Commissioner of the FCC. It took a number of steps, with each following much the same routine: Bill would contact Commissioner Lee, indicating what we needed to have authorized, and Commissioner Lee would respond, stating the electronic measurements and data which needed to be provided and the specific wording to be included in a telegram. Within a day or two of submission, we'd receive a telegram of approval in return.

The station was being constructed for broadcasting in FM stereo, which the FCC had just authorized a few weeks earlier on June 1, 1961. It was Bill and Bob's goal to be the first station to transmit stereo in the national capital region. Up to this time, stations had no need for presenting programming in stereo; hence, their facilities were equipped for just one channel of sound, known as monaural, and if stations had no need, equipment manufacturers certainly weren't offering such equipment.

Since there were no stereo studio control consoles readily available, Bob had the options of either acquiring an existing unit and rebuilding it for two channels or simply starting from scratch; Bob chose the latter. Then, there was the issue of how to generate the stereo signal needed for feeding the transmitter. Again, none of the equipment manufacturers had begun manufacturing these stereo-generating devices—at least not at a price Bill and Bob could afford. If you've not yet gathered from what I've written, WHFS was being constructed on a shoestring budget! The answer was to turn to the prominent maker of high-fidelity systems and FM receivers of the day, the H. H. Scott Company. They had created a stereo generator unit for use in testing FM stereo receivers as they came off their production line. It did exactly what was needed; it provided the desired stereo signal that Bob could interface with the input of our transmitter.

As you might imagine, the WHFS call letters were chosen by Bill and Bob, standing for "Washington's High-Fidelity Station." However, by the time we began broadcasting the letter "S" translated to "stereo." Furthermore, all music heard on WHFS was from stereo recordings, both long-play albums and prerecorded stereo tapes.

Immediately upon completing my military obligations, I began working on assembling a record library based on Bill and Bob's guidelines for what they wanted to offer the market; what you'd call a potpourri format—not something you'd likely find anywhere today, and something that had pretty much disappeared from the radio dial even then. However, they wanted to showcase FM stereo across a fair portion of the musical spectrum and offer programming that wasn't widely available on radio.

While stereo long-play recordings were quite new in their own right, with the first ones having been released less than four years earlier, the major record companies in the classical and other idioms we were interested in—especially Columbia, London, and RCA Victor—quickly dug into their vaults for performances that had been recorded in stereo, releasing stereo discs along with monaural ones that were already on the market. Also, an orchestra leader named Enoch Light organized Command Records and began releasing albums of popular melodies which accentuated the breadth of stereo sound. This allowed us to gather a sizable repertoire before our launch date of November 12, 1961. The first stereo long-play recordings were released in 1957, and the availability of both versions continued for several years, but the monaural pressings were pretty much phased out by the mid-1960s.

How did I know what to order? In my earlier years, I had had some exposure to and interest in the more popular compositions from the lighter side of the classical spectrum, plus I'd had the few months of playing classical recordings on KBIC in Thule. I presume that Bill Tynan, who was the more musically inclined of the two, also gave me a list of some of his favorites. Otherwise, I turned to the Schwann catalog, a publication that had begun in 1949 with the dawning of long-play albums, which listed virtually all available recordings of classical music. This monthly guide proved to be a trustworthy resource, since if there were two or more recordings of a particular composition, it was likely more worthy of airplay than one of which there was only a single recording.

Although I was not totally familiar with how to pronounce the names of the conductors, artists, and composers in the classical music world, I fortunately came across a pronunciation guide that was created by, I believe, the American Society of Composers, Authors and Publishers (ASCAP).

Our initial broadcast hours were 4:00 p.m. to midnight. Except for a half-hour of "ping-pong" at 7:30 each evening, our schedule up until 10:00 p.m. on weekdays featured classical and light classical recordings. Other than an occasional bit of weather information, our only deviation from music was a short stock market report aired just before 6:00 p.m. each business day. To obtain the content for this report I would dash up the street to a local brokerage office during a musical selection, pick up the information, then come back and prepare the report for reading on the air.

Beginning at 10:00 p.m. each weeknight, WHFS presented two hours of contemporary jazz, a program hosted by a local radio personality and musician named Tom Phillips. His primary work was in commercial real estate at this time in his life, but he longed to continue doing some radio, which proved to be a perfect situation for him. As for recordings for this program, Tom chose the albums we would acquire, plus he'd often bring in recordings from his own vast collection.

After we'd been in operation about a year, two decisions were made. The first was that beginning the broadcast day at noon would enhance our image and possibly grow our listenership while not greatly increasing our operating expenses. The second was that offering a monthly printed program guide listing all of the major music performances scheduled would be of interest to our growing audience. Hence, midway through 1962 we created *Stereo Notes*, which listeners could subscribe to for the grand sum of $2.00 a year.

Two notes related to our weekend programming: First, the Sunday night opera performances were aired exclusively from prerecorded four-track reel-to-reel tapes that were being released by the record companies along with the LP disc recordings. In my recollection, these stereo tapes actually became available a few years prior to the

WHFS "Stereo Notes"

appearance of stereo LPs and were sought by music lovers seeking top-notch audio quality, as the tapes usually possessed less surface noise than did the discs. The Saturday evening schedule included the airing of a full Broadway show recording, followed by the Dixieland side of jazz in a program called *Le Jazz Hot*. Leading off the evening at 7:30, the station offered an hour of comedy and other light-hearted recordings on a program we called *Just for Laughs*.

In keeping with this theme, one Saturday evening I chose to air *Stan Freberg Presents the United States of America*. Stan was known for his comedy recordings during the 1950s and 1960s, and this was his take on the early years of our nation's history, featuring music and dialogue as could only be written by Stan. I don't believe the announcer on duty on that Saturday evening received any telephone calls; however, on Monday I received calls from representatives of the Daughters of the

American Revolution complaining that we were making fun of the country's history and promising a boycott against the station. However, no such boycott occurred.

Since our broadcast control system was designed and built to do only one thing, i.e., send programming to the transmitter, for practical purposes all voice heard on the air was live. The operational center consisted of the control console, two turntables and two four-track reel-to-reel tape decks—used primarily for our Sunday evening opera broadcasts—and two microphones.

I don't believe that we ever generated enough revenue to actually cover expenses. Most of our advertising came from the stores in the Washington area that sold hi-fi equipment and/or stereo recordings and were supporting us because we were providing them with a live demonstration source for FM stereo receivers. One of our unfortunate limitations was that WHFS was operating with low

FM DIAL CARD		
WAMU	88.5	Washington, D.C.
WGTB	90.1	Washington, D.C.
WGTS	91.9	Takoma Park, Md.
WSID-FM	92.3	Baltimore, Md.
WRFL	92.9	Winchester, Va.
WFMM	93.1	Baltimore, Md.
WRC-FM	93.9	Washington, D.C.
WJMD	94.7	Bethesda, Md. (part stereo)
WRBS	95.1	Baltimore, Md.
WPGC-FM	95.5	Oakland, Md.
WTOP-FM	96.3	Washington, D.C.
WASH	97.1	Washington, D.C. (part stereo)
WBAL-FM	97.9	Baltimore, Md.
WOL-FM	98.7	Washington, D.C.
WNAV-FM	99.1	Annapolis, Md.
WGAY	99.5	Washington, D.C.
WFMD-FM	99.9	Frederick, Md.
WJAN	100.3	Washington, D.C.
WWDC-FM	101.1	Washington, D.C.
WAQE-FM	101.9	Baltimore, Md. (part stereo)
W-H-F-S	102.3	ALL STEREO
WCAO-FM	102.7	Baltimore, Md.
WGMS-FM	103.5	Washington, D.C.
WSMD	104.1	Waldorf, Md.
WITH-FM	104.3	Baltimore, Md.
WAVA-FM	105.1	Arlington, Va.
WXRA	105.9	Woodbridge, Va.
WCBM-FM	106.5	Baltimore, Md.
WPRW-FM	106.7	Manassas, Va.
WMAL-FM	107.3	Washington, D.C.
WXTC	107.9	Annapolis, Md.

A listing of Washington-Baltimore area FM stations by frequency, as printed in the back of the WHFS "Stereo Notes" program guide. (You'll read more about FM station dial cards as this book goes along—this is just the beginning.)

power and a not-very-tall antenna, and, because of a ridge of land that runs across the outer edge of northwest Washington, we weren't able to place a good signal into the heart of the city.

With the arrival of 1963, after a solid twenty months of giving my all to building and operating the station, it became evident there was not a lot more that I could do to push the station toward becoming self-supporting and profitable; furthermore, Bill and Bob were not in a position to take on added costs, such as moving the transmitter to improve the station's coverage or employing additional personnel, including one or more qualified salespersons. I loved working with the two of them and enjoyed the pioneering things we were doing with the station, but I had a wife and child and another one on the way. I felt it was time to explore other avenues where my growing range of experiences and demonstrated talents could be utilized to provide increased compensation for better support of my family. It did not take much searching to locate and secure that next position, taking me back to an area I was familiar with and not far from where I grew up.

Within months of my departure, the station would be sold and enter upon a few years of rough sailing, with changes of ownership and management. In the next couple of years, at least two high-rise apartment buildings would go up within a couple of blocks of our original location at 8218 Wisconsin Avenue in Bethesda and the station would move to one of those. This allowed its antenna to be placed on the roof, giving it a good 200 feet in increased height and far better coverage of the entire metropolitan area. Eventually, the station would find a new solid footing, and by 1968, be on its way to becoming one of the legendary stations in the free-form "progressive rock" music realm that took hold on FM in the second half of the 1960s, a format genre born in San Francisco just a year earlier in 1967.

CHAPTER 5
The Road to Philadelphia

As was the case with WHFS, my next opportunity came at another not-yet-operating station, which again I discovered through reading a broadcast industry publication. In this case, it was *Broadcasting* Magazine's Yearbook. This annual publication listed all radio and TV stations in North America which were in operation or had received permits for construction. Having grown up in the suburbs of the city, I was always interested in radio activities in the Philadelphia area. One day in February of 1963 as I perused the listings, I noted a new set of call letters, WDVR, with a frequency of 101.1 on FM. The only name listed under personnel was "David L. Kurtz, President."

With the possibility that the two principal owners of WHFS would be selling the station and my desire to return to home territory, it was time for action–to search out this possible new opportunity. It was not difficult to obtain a telephone number for Mr. Kurtz, so on my next trip to visit family in Bucks County, which borders Philadelphia on the north, I made contact with him. Hearing of my background and that I had played a major role in launching WHFS as a new station, he was most happy to have me come visit him.

After we told each other about our backgrounds—his was as an electronics engineer for the military division of the Philco Corporation—he took me over to see the completely built station, which was ready to broadcast. It only awaited a staff to create programming and man the operation. Much like WHFS, it was to be a shoestring, boot-strap operation. The biggest difference between the two physically was that WDVR's setup had four rooms and slightly more square footage.

Before the evening ended, I had been hired as the station manager and program director, based on my experience of playing much the same roles in launching WHFS as a brand-new FM station two years earlier in the Washington, D.C., market. The only issue left up in the air was what we'd program. Dave had thought it would be a good idea to accept paid religious programming to air during the morning hours to help cover expenses. While I agreed that there needed to be income generated fairly quickly, I wasn't enthralled with the thought, as it wouldn't allow for consistency of content throughout the day. But I had not yet given the matter deep consideration. However, I was visualizing something that was close to where we ended up.

What inspired Dave Kurtz to build and own a radio station? Well, from what he once told me, I believe the inspiration came at least partially from an uncle named Dr. David Palmer, the grandson of Daniel David Palmer, who is recognized as founding the profession of chiropractic. He was the son as well of Colonel B. J. Palmer, who had also become a chiropractor and is given credit for growing and developing the profession into what it is today. B. J., as he was known to most who knew him, early on recognized the potential value of radio and built WOC in the Palmers' hometown of Davenport, Iowa, in 1922. Not long after, he also established WHO in Des Moines. By the late 1950s, the stations were still in the Palmer family, had added FM and TV stations in both communities, and Dr. David had taken over the management reins.

As an aside, the call letters for the Iowa stations were specifically chosen, as were many of the early call signs, and before the Mississippi River was enforced as the dividing line as to whether a station's identifier began with a "K" or a "W." As of 2015, nearly 100 years later, the two stations retain these call letters, which stand for "Wonders Of Chiropractic" and "We Help Others."

When it came time for Dave to fulfill his dream—after having banked $27,000, which was his estimate of the cost to build his station—where else should he seek a construction permit but in greater Philadelphia, since he was already living in the city.

He first applied for 100.3 but lost out to an applicant for Media, Pennsylvania, located just a few miles to the southwest of the city; Media had no licensed station, which gave them extra points with the Federal Communications Commission. That didn't stop Dave. He searched further and found the next best possibility was 101.1, which should never had been granted, as under FCC rules of the time, it was "short-spaced," meaning it was too close, mileage-wise, to New York City's WCBS-FM.

However, since they were operating with low power at the time and Dave's application proposed only 5400 watts from the roof of an old thirteen-story office building, the FCC granted a waiver and issued the permit.

While he knew he wanted to build a station like his relatives in Iowa had done, I don't believe Dave ever envisioned it becoming the huge success it became before many years passed... and the success it would continue to have for more than half a century. A side note relating to Dave that I don't think many people ever knew: Even before WDVR began operating, he had filed an application to construct a second FM station in the Reading, Pennsylvania, suburb of Shillington. I don't really know the reason it was not granted; yet it was along about the time the FCC made a number of rule changes, which likely made Dave's application unacceptable for consideration, or someone filed an application in another community which created a conflict and he chose not to proceed.

Before I continue relating this saga, let me share this: As was the case with Bill Tynan and Bob Carpenter in Bethesda and later with Arch L. Madsen, President of Bonneville International Corporation (which you'll read about in Chapter 8), I'll always be grateful for Dave placing his trust in me and giving me the opportunity to demonstrate what I could do.

It wasn't long after the station began operating that someone got a young David L. Kurtz, who was only two years older than yours truly, to sit in the operator's chair for this photograph... likely the only time he ever sat in this chair in this radio station which he alone secured the license for and had constructed. Sadly, Dave passed away in 2005 following a battle with kidney cancer, leaving behind his wife of forty-two years, Esther, whom he had married just a month after WDVR began broadcasting.

David L. Kurtz

Meanwhile, back in Bethesda, at WHFS the following week, a young man named Jerry Lee stopped by. While employed by a station in Baltimore, he was also seeking to sell stations on utilizing the Good Music programming concepts of a friend, Ted Niarhos, who operated WDBN, an FM station in Medina, Ohio, located between Cleveland and Akron.

After telling Jerry that I could state definitely that the owners would not be interested in such a format, I said I was headed to a new station in Philadelphia. He got the details, and, as only Jerry could, hustled to see Dave and got hired as sales manager.

Not many days passed before I heard from Jerry again, telling me that we'd be working together at WDVR. While, as I mentioned, Dave had some differing thoughts on programming, Jerry and I conferred and quickly agreed that a round-the-clock utility-type format of Easy Listening recordings, where we'd play just one track at a time from each individual recording presented in quarter-hour segments, had the potential for making a solid impact quickly. While a couple of other stations in the market were playing similar music some of the time, they were not consistent in their programming as WDVR would be, and that would prove to put the station on the road to long-term success.

While Jerry offered music lists and information about the format as being executed in Ohio, I didn't feel comfortable with a fair number of the albums listed. Instead, I chose to follow my own instincts and assemble a formatic structure which my intuitive senses told me the listening public was looking for. At this very moment, I felt I was where I was meant to be: a brand-new radio station in one of the largest metropolitan regions in the country, presenting a clean palette ready to be painted with great familiar melodies performed in great instrumental arrangements, providing the perfect opportunity to develop a format built around the genre of music I loved best—one small segment out of the vast musical spectrum!

Yes, by the middle of the 1950s, while I listened to Martin Block in New York City and the 950 Club from Philadelphia playing the pop songs of the day in the 1940s and some country during the Hank Williams era of the early 1950s, my primary musical tastes had settled on the type of music and recordings which constituted the instrumentally based sound we brought to Philadelphia.

The door was open for me to change the face of the format, which at the time was simply known as Good Music. Celebrating our first anniversary in May of 1964, we published a full-page newspaper ad which listed every musical selection played between 9:00 a.m. and 11:00 p.m. Featured were such names as Mantovani, Andre Kostelanetz, Chet Atkins, the Living Strings, Roger Williams, Billy Vaughn, Frank Chacksfield, and Bert Kaempfert, and it even included an occasional tune by one of the "sweet bands," as they were known, such as Sammy Kaye and Jan Garber. While the overall sound was string orchestra-based (as it still is today, some 50+ years later) and the main focus was on the popular songs of the day, we offered an eclectic mix which ranged from light classical melodies to the "Banjo Barons Play Hawaiian Melodies." At the outset, we included very few vocals, all of which were by groups such as the Ray Charles Singers and the Norman Luboff Choir.

This style of radio format did not originate with us; it had been on the air in cities like New York, Los Angeles, San Francisco and Dallas, even Cleveland and Boston, for a decade or more, and variations of it even had a minimal presence in the Philadelphia market. However, most—including a couple of small programming packagers that were in the field—were locked in another era or were too classical, or they were too big-bandish, included too many vocals of one style or another, or were simply too eclectic. Plus, many of the stations were AM only or the focus was still on the AM side even if they had an FM, which, of course, meant they were not broadcasting in stereo. As was the case with WHFS, our programming was to be 100% in stereo.

I believe another key difference was that the overall content of what we'd be offering musically was that it would be more attuned to the changing musical tastes of the 1960s, making our sound more appealing to the masses.

In those days, there was not time to create actual music playlists, so we devised a system for managing what would deliver the desired musical sound to the airwaves: (1) a logging form was pasted on the cover of each album, and I would review and determine which selections on the recording were suited for the format, note the tempo of each and so mark the chart sheet; (2) the albums were lined up in a set order on a shelf near the operators, and they'd simply work through them in order and choose a track from the next recording in line, if it contained a selection of appropriate tempo that hadn't been played too recently; (3) at time of play, the operator would note the date of play on the album's log sheet so as to control repetition. Criteria for play were established for each hour by what was called a flow chart, which set the different tempos and their order for that hour, with different charts for the various times of the day and night.

After WDVR began to get ratings and be noticed by the industry, others began to copy my musical sound and approach— and I claim it as very much mine, as no person or station influenced what I chose to program. This is the reason I was later dubbed "Father of the modern Beautiful Music format." Over the years, not only have I been asked where I went to college to study and learn how to do this, I've been asked what stations and whose formats I copied. During the late 1950s, during some evenings I'd listen to WOR-AM from New York and their program, Music From Studio X, which I believe featured mostly string orchestra recordings. While living in the Washington, D.C., area, I would listen occasionally to the other FM station licensed to Bethesda, Maryland, WJMD, which featured an all-instrumental sound. To this day, I cannot tell you whether they played strictly orchestral recordings—I don't believe they played single selections from recordings but rather played an entire side of an LP.

Meanwhile, I had not much more than a month to secure albums and assemble a library of music and to hire what in the industry are called board operators, who would play the music from LPs, one selection per disc at a time, along with record-ed station IDs and commercials. After all, we had no plans or funds to employ professional announcers in the early days; for commercials, freelance announcers would be utilized as needed.

In the period prior to our launch, a new system for airing recorded announcements was just coming into common use in radio stations, called the NAB cartridge. It was a plastic shell containing an endless loop of tape that would automatically re-cue itself after being played and could easily be inserted into and removed from a player. With Dave's approval, I purchased three of these players from a budget-priced maker of the units, Tapecaster, which was located just up the road from WHFS in Rockville, Maryland.

Just prior to our official WDVR launch on Monday, May 13, we were on the air with test programming the previous Saturday when suddenly, the meters on the transmitter became erratic and an alarm went off. It turned out that an insulator on the antenna, which was mounted on a small pole on the roof of our location at 18 West Chelten Avenue in the Germantown section of Philadelphia, had burned out. Fortunately, the contract engineer who had helped construct the station was able to jury-rig an arrangement until a replacement part arrived, allowing the station to go on as planned.

Dave was very opposed to broadcasting twenty-four hours a day, as he felt the added expense of operating overnight couldn't be justified. How did Jerry overcome this? He went out and sold two major advertisers—the Philco Corporation and one of the city's largest car dealers, John B. White Ford—on being co-sponsors of the midnight to 6:00 a.m. all-night show. Since overnight wasn't considered prime time in the advertising world, their contracts provided them with the added benefits of receiving a number of daytime announcements each day as well.

Up through the 1950s and even into the early 1960s in some cases, most radio stations did not operate twenty-four hours a day; instead, they signed off at midnight or shortly thereafter and returned to the air around 6:00 a.m., maybe 5:00 a.m. in larger metropolitan areas and in agricultural communities, where farmers got up before dawn to milk their cows. I found no record of how or when this practice became the norm, but most stations signed off and came back on by playing the "Star-Spangled Banner." Not that he wasn't patriotic, but Dave Kurtz, being a Christian gentleman from the Pennsylvania Dutch region of Lancaster County, Pennsylvania, felt that he

wanted WDVR to sign on each day with a recorded performance of the Lord's Prayer. Even though we had committed to WDVR signing on that Monday morning and never signing off again, Dave's wish was carried out by playing the Mormon Tabernacle Choir's recording of the Lord's Prayer

The recording by the Mormon Tabernacle Choir sits ready for play each morning just prior to 6 A. M.. Joaquin Bowman is at the controls. (Courtesy of Dave Shayer collection)

each and every morning at 5:58. This practice would continue daily for at least the next forty years. In later years, until it was finally dropped on November 19, 2015, it was a five-day-a-week presentation airing at 5:00 a.m., with the Prayer being sung by vocalist Aaron Neville. It's quite a record for the history books.

Well, we had survived our first equipment failure, the programming was set, the crew was in place and ready to go, and we had two advertisers signed up. So, it was time for Philadelphia's newest radio station to begin broadcasting and make a difference in the lives of tens of thousands who lived in the Delaware Valley region of Pennsylvania and New Jersey!

CHAPTER 6

May 13, 1963

That date will forever be fixed in my mind; fifty-four years ago as of this writing. We had just officially signed on WDVR, a brand-new FM station in Philadelphia, the nation's number four market at the time. And, I was beginning—whether I realized it or not—on the road to major success in my beloved field of radio broadcasting.

As I've noted, we were not the first station in the nation, or even in Philadelphia, to play a Good Music/Easy Listening format, but we were doing it in a very different way, playing a mix of melodies and sounds that was different from all the others, in what we included as well as what we excluded.

Little did I realize on that Monday morning, from the humble beginnings of a station which was operating from just four rooms on the 11th floor of an office building with a staff of six and a half people with a less-than-ideal signal, that what we were doing would quickly attract and capture the hearts of thousands. Yes, soon we would be describing it as "the little station that could!"

What was that musical sound? As a press release mailed out on that first day, May 13, stated: "Programming will be devoted exclusively to bright, familiar music with every selection easy to recognize." And, as I noted earlier, every recording played was a stereo recording. As far as I can remember, as was the case at WHFS in the Washington, D.C., area, we were the only station in the Philadelphia region which could claim that all of its programming was in FM stereo.

So, on May 13, 1963, having hired five young college-age gentlemen who desired to break into radio to play the recordings and the recorded station IDs and commercials for our first and only two advertisers, we were officially off and running!

Because these five operators—Lou, Dick, Frank, Dave, and Joaquin—had no real training or experience in announcing, their voices were not heard at all in those early days. As the weeks went by, they'd begin practicing the preparation and recording of brief weather reports, described as "weather in a word… sunny." Eventually, we began airing those reports, hourly during the morning hours of 6:00, 7:00, and 8:00 and then every three hours through the remaining twenty-one hours of the day beginning at 9:30. This began our development beyond being simply an all-recorded jukebox and conveying the message to listeners that there were real folks at the station and we knew what day and time it was.

The WDVR control room with Dave Shayer on duty. (Courtesy of Dave Shayer collection)

On the non-programming side, it wasn't long before the White Ford folks began to question the wisdom of their advertising expenditures on the station, asking how we were building our listenership, as they did not see the station doing any advertising of its own. Jerry Lee, the master promoter, conceived of a small billboard ad campaign, provided that a couple of the billboards would be strategically placed near the White Ford showroom on North Broad Street. In designing our ad, I remember Jerry specifically telling the billboard company artist that he "didn't care what typeface they used on the poster... as long as it was big block letters!"

WDVR's first billboard

By late summer of 1963, it was time to move to the next level in providing information to the listeners. In other words, to add brief news summaries to our schedule of weathercasts. Considering that we did not have funds to yet subscribe to the Associated Press teletype news service, we needed an alternative. So, we set up three radio receivers in the transmitter room, which was adjacent to the control room in our four-room station facility. Each was tuned to a different area station that had genuine news operations, one of which originated from one of Philadelphia's daily newspapers. An hour or so prior to each report, the operator would record a newscast from one of the stations and then play it back a story at a time and summarize it in one sentence for a total of about three stories. By this method, we were able to let listeners know that things were okay in the world.

That was until Friday, November 22, when President John F. Kennedy was assassinated in Dallas. Up until this time, the station had never broadcast a single word live... and we did not have the capability to go live from the control room. This made it nearly impossible for the operator on duty to handle this extreme situation of attempting to gather, prepare, and record information and keep the station running as well. The microphone in the control room was wired to feed the cartridge recorder, as the operators always prerecorded all weather and news reports, providing the opportunity for them to be redone if a major mistake was made.

At the time the first bulletins of the shooting were being broadcast by the networks, I was across town in a bank office making one of my infrequent advertising sales calls. While I was sitting with the advertising manager, his telephone rang. He answered and immediately got an alarmed look on his face. Upon hanging up, he told me what had happened and asked if I wanted to call the station. I did and was told that our morning operator at the time, Terry Wickham, had called and was on his way back to the station to help in whatever way possible.

I was immediately on my way as well, a trip that would take about thirty minutes door-to-door. What my thoughts were as I drove, I do not remember. I likely tuned into a station that was airing information about the President being shot––whether it was known at that point that he had died, I have no memory.

Knowing my thought processes, I'm sure much of my thinking was focused on what we needed to do regarding our programming and communicating to our listeners the relevant information about the shooting and what would follow.

Terry and I arrived at about the same time, and we quickly assembled the prime information and put Terry in the adjoining studio to report, as that's where we had the capability to go live. Meanwhile, I began sorting through our recordings to choose selections that were not particularly familiar and rather low key as the nation began to mourn.

By evening, Dave Kurtz had arrived with a box of classical recordings from his personal collection and re-wired the control room microphone so that it was connected to the broadcast circuit. I don't believe we ever did another recorded news report after that time, which worked out well, as our operators had gained experience and demonstrated their capabilities.

On this momentous day in history, a gentleman named Mike Strug came on duty as the WDVR evening operator/announcer. I make note of Mike because he, more than anyone in our employ that I can remember, would go on to be a well-recognized name in Philadelphia broadcasting circles, with a decades-long career as a television news field reporter.

Throughout the weekend and until the beginning of the president's state funeral proceedings on Monday morning, WDVR broadcast a mix of lighter symphonic music and selections from our regular library. Of the latter, the music of the Melachrino Orchestra seemed very suited to our needs, if my memory serves me correctly. We gained a new and different audience during this time, as Philadelphia's classical station had turned to a diet of Bach Masses and other heavy liturgical recordings, which was not to the particular liking of many of their listeners. Like most stations across the nation, we aired no commercials during this period.

During the weekend, I reached the General Manager of WRCV Radio, the NBC-owned station in Philadelphia, and gained his authorization to provide NBC Radio's coverage of this momentous day to our listeners. Unfortunately, WRCV was AM-only and we weren't able to secure a static-free signal from them; however, we were able to pick up a strong, clear signal from WDEL-FM in Wilmington, Delaware, which still simulcast its AM sister, also an NBC affiliate—which saved the day. After the president was laid to rest in Arlington National Cemetery late in the day, we, along with most other radio and TV stations, gradually returned to our regular programming.

Thanksgiving Day came later that week, marking the beginning of the Christmas season and our beginning to include holiday recordings in our mix. We began with just a few per hour, mostly just the popular holiday melodies at the outset. Then, we gradually built in quantity per hour and added in the traditional carols until Christmas Eve.

Not having any commercials to air, I conceived of calling our all-holiday music programming on Christmas Eve and Christmas Day our first annual *Christmas Festival of Music* to set it apart from our regular programming. While there might have been stations elsewhere which played a full diet of holiday-oriented music for the day-and-a-half period, I was not aware of them. Most stations that I knew, if they aired Christmas-themed programming, aired mostly hour and half-hour specialty shows.

However, by Christmas 1964, numerous stations across the country had picked up on the nonstop-music approach.

For the first couple of years, while we aired a lot of Christmas selections through the month of December, the festival did not begin until 9:00 p.m. on Christmas Eve and actually had some regular tunes mixed in by later on Christmas Day. Compare that to fifty years later, when at least one radio station in every market of any size across the country plays non-stop Christmas music for as much as six weeks leading up to Christmas.

As of this writing in late 2017, Chuck Knight is program director of 101.1 More FM in Philadelphia, the successor to WDVR. As his station has been one of those stations for many years, I asked Chuck his opinion on why the all-Christmas radio station format continues to be so popular in cities throughout America, considering that the country's population is becoming more secular and less Christian as each year passes. I found his response to be quite insightful: "I've always believed that the foundation of the holiday season is all about tradition. At almost any of our ages, the holidays are universally a trip down memory lane to a happy, simpler, and easier time. The Christmas music—secular vs. non-secular is irrelevant in this mindset—is the Pavlovian conditioning that sets in motion all of our wonderful thoughts, memories, feelings, and emotions."

The station hadn't been on the air very long when we developed the postcard-sized FM dial card concept. I'm not sure where this design came from, but as displayed in Chapter 4, in the back of our monthly WHFS *Stereo Notes* program guide was a listing of the FM stations in the greater Washington-Baltimore area under the heading FM DIAL CARD (even though it wasn't actually a card). However, at WDVR we took it mainstream, printing several hundred thousand of these "informational" items and placing them in any kind of store that sold an FM radio. Stores were happy to take them on, as they were a great tool for selling FM receivers: the salesman could point out all of the stations which could be heard on the FM band. So that the cards didn't sit loose and get knocked off the counter and wasted, Jerry had our printer develop a cardboard standup holder that held about 125 cards.

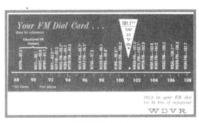
WDVR dial card

Because WDVR was already showing a decent listenership in the Hooperatings monthly reports—in fact, we quickly became the highest-rated FM station—after only a few months of broadcasting, our roster of advertisers began to grow as we went into 1964. With this new revenue, we were able to justify contracting for the Associated Press teletype news service, dispensing with the receivers in the transmitter room.

Sometime in 1964, a gentleman whose name is known to many in the radio industry, Jerry Del Colliano, came on board as one of our operator/announcers. From WDVR, Jerry went on to successful positions as a radio station program director, industry newsletter publisher, and college professor. Today, he is a consultant to numerous stations and organizations which deal with a variety of media challenges. In a recent exchange, Jerry said about yours truly: "I have never seen anyone more methodical or detailed about putting out a good product."

In these early days of WDVR, it was a learning experience for all of us. Other than working with three or four part-time announcers at WHFS, all of whom had more radio experience than me, I had never managed anyone. Yet, I intuitively knew what the station needed to sound like, and it was my job to mentor, guide, and train this group of young guys—many of whom were students at Temple University's Communications School—in how to select and play the recordings and to prepare our two-minute newscasts so as to deliver the maximum amount of meaningful information in this short span of time. Also, it was an ongoing process, as we'd have changes in our crew as the months passed. So, to have Jerry remember me in this way some fifty-plus years later is truly heart-warming.

I'm sure other program directors were doing this and still do today: I'd sleep with a radio playing the station softly by my side of the bed. It was amazing how often I'd awaken just as the operator on duty was going "astray"; in one case, there was dead air, and two or three other times I caught him allowing an entire side of an album to play.

As the months passed, it became obvious that we needed to have an experienced announcer on staff to handle the growing number of commercials that needed to be recorded. I began a search by listening to stations in outlying areas surrounding Philadelphia, listening for voices that I felt would be compatible with our format. I eventually settled on approaching Phil Stout, who was working at WTOA, an independent FM station in Trenton. I finally convinced Phil that making a move to WDVR would be a solid step up, and he joined us in late 1964.

Other than working with the air staff, I devoted much time

to searching out new recordings to find selections for enlarging our library, as it was vital to maintain a freshness in our sound and avoid any hint of repetition. The record industry has always employed people to call on radio stations to push their latest releases in the hopes of gaining airplay, which would boost record sales. Since the kind of music and albums we were seeking did not match what they were promoting, none of these folks ever came to WDVR. So, I developed a routine of visiting the four key record distributors in Philadelphia from time to time and rummaging through their warehouse shelves to find new material by our type of artists.

On the subject of music, I remember receiving a call one day from a listener asking about a recording that had just played. After I told him it was the Hollyridge Strings playing "Michelle," I happened to mention it was a Beatles tune. You could hear his horrified silent shock reverberate through the phone! The Beatles were still quite new to the world at this time and older individuals, who didn't care for the group's sound and what was simply called "rock music," hadn't yet realized how great many of their melodies were, even if they didn't care for the original performances.

While I have an entire chapter devoted to many of the unique recordings that became great favorites of our millions of listeners across the land, there were two musical selections which we played during these early years that I want to make note of: one proved to be much loved, while the other struck a highly negative chord. During this time in the early 1960s, pianist George Greeley produced a series of LPs with the Warner Brothers Symphony Orchestra. We played several songs from them, yet the one that particularly caught our listeners' fancy was the Love Music from Richard Wagner's opera, *Tristan und Isolde*. It's a long selection, running more than five minutes, which is far longer than our limit for any of our recordings. (In later years, when we began airing the musical programming from tape, we edited the front portion—the least exciting part of the composition—and it's still being played today on Sirius XM's Escape channel.)

Then there's the one that quickly became one of the few recordings I've programmed over the years that became a negative for a group of listeners... twice! *Il Silenzio* (*The Silence*) is a piece notable for its theme being played by a trumpet, while its melody is an extension of the Italian Cavalry bugle call used by the Russian composer Tchaikovsky to open his *Capriccio Italien*, often mistaken for the U.S. military bugle call "Taps"— and that was the rub. After the 101 Strings released a recording of the tune, I listened and found it very appealing, so I began to play it. However, it wasn't long before the station began receiving telephone calls from women who were wives, mothers, or girlfriends of men who had died in military service. The message was the same in every case: "please don't play that, I find it too painful to hear." It didn't take many calls for me to realize it was not a recording that we should continue playing.

After we had launched the format on XM Radio in 2002, I came across Paul Mauriat's recording of the same tune. Thinking that times and circumstances might have changed, I tried inserting it into the schedule. It took only a couple of plays for us to hear from a couple of women expressing the same feelings that we'd heard some forty years earlier. That was it; I would never program *Il Silenzio* again.

Before I leave the subject of music, let me share something that was happening that I discovered after it had apparently been going on for some time. I will not mention a name so as to protect the guilty, and no, I did not fire the person. One day, I realized there were at least a couple of albums that were no longer in our lineup. *Where did they go?* I wondered. Something told me, or maybe I was tipped off–I don't remember now. I looked in the drop ceiling above the operator's chair in the control room, and inside were at least a half-dozen LP recordings, all normally in our album rotation! Of course, this was his way of not having to play selections from these albums that he didn't care for. And, yes, we did put them back into play.

Another of my WDVR duties was the scheduling of commercials, a position typically called "traffic manager." For the first several years, WDVR limited its commercials to four per hour. This was not a challenge for the first year of operation, maybe even well into the second. However, as the station grew in popularity, we started receiving orders through advertising agencies. Back then, most agency folks still thought in terms of AM radio and people being in their cars driving home from work, known as the afternoon commute. With this philosophy, most of them wrote their clients' contracts stipulating that the commercials must air between 4:00 and 7:00 p.m., to reach those during the time they'd supposedly most likely be listening. Under our strict policy, we had room for only thirteen commercials each day. So, it wasn't long before I was deeply into the "fudge" game, i.e., deciding which commercials I could get away with slotting in at 7:15 or 3:45 or even 3:30.

Advertising sales continued to grow, but month after

month, we just couldn't break through the $10,000-per-month level. Then, we suddenly jumped to something like $13,000, and the station has barely ever paused to look back at any time over these past fifty-plus years!

In 1965, a new company named American Research Bureau entered the radio audience ratings field and surveyed the country's major markets during the fall of that year. The results showed that WDVR had a higher average listenership than any other FM station in the nation. In a full-page ad published in the Philadelphia Inquirer on Thursday, December 9, the station announced:

WDVR IS NOW THE
NO. 1 FM STATION
IN THE ENTIRE NATION

This means that WDVR outranks every FM station in New York, Chicago, Los Angeles, or any other FM station in the country.

And, not long afterward, this announcement was followed by this billboard:

With the arrival of 1966, the station had cemented its position as a major player in the Philadelphia radio community and was attracting more and more advertisers. Phil Stout had demonstrated his skills not just as an announcer but as someone who could choose new recordings and manage the programming, and we had a fairly stable crew of announcer/operators. Was it time for Marlin to seek new territory to conquer?

CHAPTER 7

New England Years

By the spring of 1966, WDVR had been on the air for three years and had achieved several FM station milestones, not just in Philadelphia but on a national level as well. And when a routine begins to take on a sameness, I start to become bored and restless.

It was time for a new challenge, which came again through a listing in *Broadcasting* magazine. This time it was in the form of a classified ad for the position of General Manager & Program Director for the Concert Network's two classical music-oriented stations, WBCN in Boston, Massachusetts, and WHCN in Hartford, Connecticut. Being eager for opportunities where I believed I could bring about a turnaround and overcome the odds, I jumped on this one, feeling that programming classical music was not tremendously different from programming the pop-oriented music we aired on WDVR. I had programmed the format at WHFS in Bethesda and before that during part of my Army tour in Greenland and had an intuitive understanding of how to best present the genre on radio, including the prime composers and compositions to feature.

Even though it had a classically programmed competitor which was doing well, WCRB, I felt the heritage was there and that WBCN had simply gotten off track because the former program director had taken the station's music in a very esoteric direction, which drove away listeners. And, I believed that Boston, with its plethora of colleges and population makeup, could support two classical stations.

However, I did not take the time to investigate matters sufficiently to realize that I would be jumping into a chaotic situation and dealing with one of the all-time eccentrics in the history of radio, T. Mitchell Hastings. "Mitch," as he was universally known, was an engineering genius who is credited with developing the first FM receiver for the automobile as well

T. Mitchell Hastings
(Courtesy of Sam
Kopper collection)

as an early pocket transistor FM radio before turning to radio broadcasting in 1958. It was then that he created a five-station group in New England and New York named the Concert Network. However, by 1966 only two stations remained; WBCN in Boston and WHCN in Hartford.

Our arrangement as laid out by Mitch was that I would oversee programming and the general overall station management and that Mitch would focus on developing advertising sales, where he was "well qualified with many connections."

Together we'd bring WBCN (WHCN was being totally ig-nored at this point; it had one person who played tapes from WBCN several hours a day to maintain its license) to financial and rating success.

Before I share the details of the saga that was to unfold, let me digress for a moment. Joaquin Bowman, one of the team of operators/announcers during the early years of WDVR, and I had the good fortune to meet again some thirty years later when we both were living in Doylestown, Pennsylvania. During a recent conversation, he called me "courageous." That is a term I never thought about as applying to me, but his reason-ing was that I was willing to risk jumping from the secure sit-uation I had at WDVR to this position which possessed many unknowns in another city.

Roy Williams, known as the Wizard of Ads and founder of the Wizard Academy on a hilltop outside Austin, Texas, has said that "Courage is to have such security in your identity that you're willing to risk open failure." Whether I fit Roy Williams' description, I'm not sure; in my case, it might have been fool-ishness, since I had a wife and three young children to support!

Unfortunately, by the time I arrived with family in tow and began my work, I found that, in true Mitch style, the scenario had changed. My chief focus was to be growing revenues. However, this immediately presented three obstacles: (1) sales has never been my forte; (2) I did not know the market from a business/sales aspect, plus no qualified radio salesperson had any desire to work for WBCN or Mitch, as they saw it as a losing proposi-tion, and (3) without a mass improvement in the programming, we had no hope of attracting new listeners or advertisers.

However, I was able to sign up one advertiser in short order. The Evelyn Wood Reading Dynamics, a speed reading training program which was very popular in the 1960s, would sign a one-year contract with most any station that had a listener demographic makeup which they believed were potential customers. The typical contract, as in WBCN's case, was for a year but only at $100 a week; if the station delivered, the budget increased. This, unfortunately in our case, was not the end of the story. Even though the company badly needed revenue, before the contract could even begin, Mitch had visited the local Evelyn Wood center and changed the terms to one-half cash and one-half in trade for enrollment of his children!

My first order of business was to begin reconstructing the programming to bring the content into a mainstream, broadly popular lineup of classical works, a 180-degree shift from a schedule of compositions where anything by Beethoven, Tchaikovsky, or similar popular composers was not included, as they had been deemed to be nothing more than junk, in the realm of contemporary rock and roll tunes.

I never knew if Mitch had no understanding of classical music or proper programming, or if he just didn't pay any attention. In any case, it didn't take long to realize the challenges were far greater than I had imagined. For example, there was a fifteen-minute broadcast each morning at 8:00 by Brother Mandus, a Christian evangelist that Mitch and his wife Margot had met and become enamored with while on a visit to England–a complete disruption in the regular programming.

I'd been there no more than a month and had completed laying out in detail the modified classical programming and getting it on the air when Mitch came bouncing back into the station one afternoon and called me into his office. He couldn't wait to tell me that he'd just finished meeting with two owners of an advertising agency who saw that the real future for the station, especially with me there, lay in a shift to Easy Listening and dropping classical music. Mitch saw this as the vision he'd been seeking, and a date had been set for the changeover.

In any other situation and with any other ownership, this could have been a brilliant strategy, as was proven just a year later by another station. But in Mitch's case, there were always strings attached. For WBCN, it would not be a twenty-four-hour-a-day change. There'd still be a three-hour block of classical weekday evenings plus certain hours on the weekends, as these were tied to long-term sponsorship contracts, plus there'd still be Brother Mandus in the mornings. A part of the irony here was that these disruptors of the new format did not produce any cash revenue—they were deals that traded service in return for advertising. A small portion covered some station operating needs, but most went to services and perks for Mitch and his family.

My next challenge was to gather a library of Easy Listening recordings in short order and get them programmed into a decent-sounding format while dealing with a rather uncooperative staff, who were there because they loved classical music, not this new format of music, for which they had minimal empathy. I later learned, as was quoted in the book written about WBCN by Boston radio personality Carter Alan, that Ron Della Chiesa and the classical format announcers there at the time I arrived in 1966 believed that I had conceived the whole plan of converting the station's format. In reality, I was as shocked as the air guys when Mitch made the announcement.

Another interesting aspect of working for Mitch and the Concert Network was that payday was on Thursday–except when it wasn't! I quickly learned that our paychecks would be delivered when Leslie, the business manager, arrived at the station, which meant that there were sufficient funds in the bank to cover the payroll. If we were lucky, that would be later on Thursday or Friday morning. Some weeks, though, it was not until the following Monday.

Another interesting aside was that the Internal Revenue Service had an interest in the finances of the Concert Network, Inc. I never understood why, as it was obvious that the company was not profitable. Possibly it was related to all of the perks the Hastings family was reaping from the operation. The funny side of this story was that an agent would set up an appointment with Mitch for 1:00 p.m. on Monday afternoon. Right on schedule, the agent would arrive at our offices on Newberry Street in Boston's Back Bay section. However, there'd be no Mitch. Someone would start calling in search of him and find that he was not even in Boston nor even nearby–he'd still be at the Hastings' weekend and summer home on Martha's Vineyard! If this had been a one-time incident, it could be chalked up to Mitch's forgetting. But the same scenario played out multiple timcs. This was true T. Mitchell Hastings. He did not forget these appointments; this was his way of dealing with the IRS–agree to meet the agent but simply not show up!

Since the station was not profitable–WHCN had zero revenue–Mitch had a constant job of coming up with monies to keep it on the air. This mostly was achieved by selling new shares of stock to his "old boys' club" friends and a few new unsuspecting individuals he encountered.

Back to our chronological timeline: In less than a month's time, we'd acquired a new record library, I'd structured a new format once again and laid out the initial days of programming and WBCN had made the transition to the new format. Meanwhile, the men advising Mitch had found an experienced Boston radio sales representative, Leonard Cohen, who was willing to take on the challenge of selling advertising on this old station with a new musical format. At the same time, I found a staff member who I felt had a feel for what we were attempting to do, so I placed him in charge of the daily music scheduling.

This gave me time to investigate the potential for WHCN finding success in the Hartford market, as there was not yet an Easy Listening station there. Funds did not exist for the station to begin operating around the clock, but we were able to extend the broadcast day from six to fifteen hours.

This was truly a shoestring operation, as the station had no offices or studios as such—the complete operation including the transmitter consisted of two rooms in a stone building sitting on top of a large hill outside of Meriden, Connecticut, situated midway between Hartford and New Haven. Because this peak also was the location for the antennas and transmitters of three other FM stations and one TV station, it had been dubbed Radio Mountain.

A few months after WHCN's conversion from classical to an instrumentally based Easy Listening genre, when we had begun to get some traction and were picking up listeners, we ex-

perienced a major transmitter failure. Considering the company's precarious financial condition, barely allowed them to keep
the stations operating, I knew that repairing WHCN's transmitter–which could involve a major expenditure–was not going to
be a priority item. So again, I was seeking a new opportunity.

Fortunately, at that moment, WLAE-FM, which shared the
building with WHCN and aired a truly eclectic version of an
Easy Listening format, had need for both a weekend announcer and a sales rep. As noted earlier, sales was not my calling, but
I did manage to sign a couple of advertisers. One was a flight
instruction school offering pilot training, which experienced
great results and had to cancel because they couldn't handle
any more students.

Before I leave the subject of WBCN, I want to share that
WBCN and its call letters would go on to secure legendary status in the annals of broadcasting, not as a classical music station,
but rather in the free-form "progressive rock" music realm, as
did my former Washington, D.C., station, WHFS. Radio Free
Boston launched during the overnight hours on WBCN beginning on March 15, 1968, and would eventually expand to dom-
inate the station's full schedule, taking the Concert Network to
profitability for the first time in its history.

While this move to New England had so far not proven to
be an astute one, the skies were about to brighten. Fortunately
for the welfare of my family, not too many weeks passed after the
WHCN debacle before I had a call from my longtime industry
friend, Bob Richer, telling me that Kaiser Broadcasting had purchased an FM station in Boston which was to be formatted sim-
ilarly to WDVR and that my programming services would be

needed and desired. Bob did not work for Kaiser, but he was to be its national advertising sales representative in New York. His agreement with them included a stipulation that the station's programming be under my supervision. I was most thankful for Bob's intervention on my behalf and am still thankful to him for his support. It was time to pack up and move back to Beantown, where we'd moved from just eight months earlier, and begin another chapter in my lifelong journey, where my goal, my mission has never changed: to make a difference in people's lives through what I bring to the airwaves.

It was now August of 1967, and considering that Boston was a waterfront city, WJIB was to have a nautical theme. The call letters, JIB, were in reference to one of

WJIB sign

the sails on a sailboat, and the station was set to launch at 12:00 a.m. on September 15. Its audio signature was a ship's bell, which would be heard at the top of each hour, ringing off the hours as based on naval tradition. Adding to our image, the studios and offices were situated at the end of Commercial Wharf, which extended out into Boston harbor not far from historic Faneuil Hall.

With just over a month to go before sign-on, my major challenge was again to secure a library of recordings sufficient for creating a musical sound that would put the station's best foot forward. At the same time, WJIB's general manager, Peter Taylor (no relation to me nor to the Taylor family, owners of the *Boston Globe* newspaper and part-owners of WJIB), was busy hiring an air staff, and the engineers were constructing the broadcast facilities.

Everything was going smoothly until the evening of September 14, when the engineers were feverishly working to complete the one control room that the station would have as we began operations. The schedule was a little tight, but the last wire was put in place at 11:50 p.m., with ten minutes to spare!

WJIB did debut on schedule at midnight and was manned by live announcer-operators who worked in four- to six-hour shifts. Just as was done at WDVR, the music was played directly from long-play recordings, one selection at a time, meaning that the person on duty was kept busy changing records.

This would prove to be a tumultuous year for Boston radio. Just months earlier, in February of 1967, the 50,000-watt old-line block-programmed AM station WNAC shook up the market by transforming itself into WRKO 680 AM, airing a Bill Drake Top 40 hits music format. And WJIB was about to do it again, yet for a whole different segment of the populace. Then, as noted earlier, the Boston radio market would be rocked again just six months later with the arrival of Radio Free Boston at WBCN in March of 1968.

As was the case with the other two stations/formats, WJIB was an immediate hit, and letters to the editors of area newspapers declared it to be one of the best things to ever happen in Boston radio. For instance, less than a month after sign-on, a letter from a gentleman in Bennington, New Hampshire, appeared in the *Globe*: "We in New Hampshire wish to thank the Kaiser-Globe FM station WJIB for the many, many pleasant hours we have spent listening to your good music. It is very rare one can get so much of it continuously and we enjoy it more than we can say. I've told all my friends who have stereos, and I am sure they all are listening."

During those early weeks, we received many comments about our lack of commercials. This was a philosophical approach taken by Kaiser Broadcasting: to have the station operate commercial-free for its first ninety days. In fact, not a single salesperson was to be hired until the new year. However, the station's popularity grew so rapidly that adverting agencies were knocking on our door, seeking to buy announcements for their clients, even before the ninety-day period had ended.

Why did WJIB achieve such dramatic overnight success when WBCN, just fifteen months earlier, had begun playing virtually the same music on FM and saw little in the way of an influx of listenership? While WJIB had the benefit of new call letters, favorable publicity, and a consistent around-the-clock format, WBCN was still saddled with the classical music image that hung on as a result of not dropping the classical block at night. Additionally, it was saddled with those old, familiar call letters that said "classical music." What publicity it received in the newspapers placed more focus on the dropping of classical than it did on the new format and what its genre was.

The advertising agency folks who advised Mitch Hastings to make the format switch were certainly correct in recommending the Good Music format, as the AM station, WEZE, which was programming within the genre, was an easy target to knock off—as WJIB would quickly prove. It was overloaded with news and commercials, and its music was dated, leaning more into the light classical realm rather than playing great instrumental arrangements of the wonderfully popular melodies of the mid-20th century. I was not present for the meeting, but

I'm sure there were caveats placed on what was required in making WBCN's format change, which Mitch chose not to hear.

As the general manager of WBCN, it was my job to put a positive spin on the change, even though my inner spirit told me there wasn't much hope. If Mitch had accepted and facilitated the dropping of the classical music entirely—which came about less than three years later—as well as a change of call letters, I would have stayed in Boston and worked day and night to gain the success we had in Philadelphia. At WDVR, we did not have a bundle of dollars either, only what we could have had at WBCN: a consistent, around-the-clock format and image and new call letters, plus commitment, passion, and a guerrilla attitude!

Fifty years later, I can conjecture that if I had by that point gained a little more of the managerial maturity that became evident just a couple of years later, I could have brought forth and helped achieve a better outcome. Possibly we could have convinced the nighttime sponsors to accept a change in the musical content while keeping their time block sponsorships intact. Also, maybe Mitch would have allowed us to move Brother Mandus to 5:45 a.m., a time I could have lived with. But what transpired, other than a few months of rough sailing for my family and myself, could not have yielded a better outcome for the years that followed.

If the station was hampered because of call letters that said "classical music" and had a block of hours that denied consistency in formatting and no budget for advertising, then how did the station succeed with its part-time Radio Free Boston free-form rock music format? Simple: Not only were there thousands of young people in Boston who were hungry to hear this music on the radio, there was a network of clubs and print publications focused on this music and the artists, so it was easy to spread the word.

It was about this time that Jim Schulke concluded that the only way they were going to get the quality and consistency of programming necessary in order for stations to achieve significant ratings was for them to create and package the programming. Jim was the co-owner with Bob Richer of the national advertising sales representative firm, Quality Media, Inc., which represented both WJIB and WDVR. Jim came to me, asking that I record segments of my music as it played on WJIB. To do so, he provided me with a small Sony reel-to-reel tape deck and a batch of seven-inch reels of tape.

This was in December 1967, and early in the new year, they were ready to hire a music programmer and begin recording tapes. All they needed was the perfect person to fill that role... "Who, Marlin, can you recommend?"

Well, I did not have a wide collection of contacts and knew only one person who understood the philosophy and had worked with programming the music "Marlin's way"; that was Phil Stout, who had taken over as my replacement at WDVR. After convincing Jim and Bob that Phil was the one person I could recommend, it then fell to me to convince Phil that this was an opportunity he should latch on to, which he did in February of 1968.

Around the same time, I incurred the wrath of Kaiser Broadcasting's president, Richard C. "Dick" Block, by allowing myself to be quoted in an industry trade publication. I don't remember what the subject was; it was not a major item or quote and did not provide anyone with any proprietary information;

however, only Mr. Block could speak under the Kaiser name, which I did not speak for, I just happened to be employed by. At the same time, Dick was in tune with so much of what was happening, even in music—having called me one day to recommend that I play Paul Mauriat's great recording "Love Is Blue," long before it was receiving any real radio industry attention.

In the first few months of 1968, I made at least three visits to sister station KFOG in San Francisco, whose studios sat above Ghirardelli Square and had a view of Alcatraz. We made several adjustments in the programming but were not as successful as in Boston. This was mostly because their competitor, KABL, was a better-programmed station than WEZE, and secondarily because KFOG management was not committed to carrying through on the changes I deemed necessary.

I don't know who was chosen to replace Phil at WDVR, but the replacement was not working out. Plus, while I was not aware of it prior to my return, there were other internal operational issues that were worsening with each passing day.

Just eight months after my arrival at the station, with WJIB already a major ratings success, Jerry Lee called to say they were experiencing some difficulties back in Philadelphia and asked whether I would consider returning. So, with Kaiser Broadcasting's *dramatic* increase in compensation demonstrating that they really didn't value my contribution to WJIB's success very highly, exactly two years after my heading north to Boston, I returned to WDVR as Program Director and Station Operations Manager in May of 1968.

CHAPTER 8

From Beantown to the City of Brotherly Love to the Big Apple

When I returned to WDVR to again take responsibility for its programming and operations, it was not to the same building that I had left two years earlier. In that span of time, the station had moved from the small space in the old Philadelphia neighborhood of Germantown to larger quarters in a new office building on City Line Avenue adjacent to the facilities of two of the city's major TV stations, plus it had arranged to improve its marginal signal by moving to one of the towers in Philadelphia's TV antenna farm. Also in this two-year period, there'd been a nearly 100% turnover in the staff along with an increase in number, mostly on the sales and marketing side. So, Jerry Lee and founder and principal owner Dave Kurtz were the only people I really knew.

I should also note that not long after my departure two years earlier, Dave had appointed Jerry to be general manager and they had worked out an agreement whereby for each year that the station met preset goals for increases in revenue and profits, Jerry would acquire an additional percentage of corporate ownership, up to 49.9 per cent.

In programming, the music had begun to skew off in a direction that was making the station less appealing, with the listener ratings suffering as a result. Though I don't remember a lot of details, I know that the musical sound had become rather lackluster and repetitious and had a sameness song after song—a direction an inexperienced programmer tends to go when feeling a need to play it safe. Hence, this was the first issue to be addressed.

The solution was to reinstate recordings which had been removed after I had left in 1966 and search out new recordings in order to restore variety in instrumentation, arrangement, and tempo. I remember listening to the station after instituting these changes and feeling a concern that I'd brightened the overall sound too much. Yet when the next ratings report arrived, it showed WDVR as having some of the strongest audience numbers up to that time. Hallelujah!

There were discipline and presentational issues to be addressed as well, considering that the operating crew had been upgraded and it was apparent that they'd not had much supervision and guidance. This was a music station with minimum talk, which required effective editing and scripting of news and weathercasts.

All of this called for regular monitoring of the on-air presentation, as you could never be sure of exactly what you'd hear. For example, not long after my return, I was listening late one evening and found the evening host's voice slightly slurred. To explain this, I must back up and tell you that in constructing the station's new facilities, Jerry Lee included a small bar that the sales team could use for entertaining potential clients during tours of the station. At all other times, the room was kept securely locked and most of the staff, including yours truly, did not have a key or access (not that I ever cared to indulge). However, there had been an emergency key hidden somewhere and our evening host had somehow located it and was helping himself during his air shift when no one else was around. As you can guess, as of the end of his air shift—or maybe sooner, I don't remember—he joined the ranks of the unemployed!

Another situation had developed which brought about the first expansion of my duties: the office folks were getting slower and slower in getting the bills for advertising mailed out. Of course, this greatly slowed the dollars coming in; dollars that were very much needed to cover operating costs. It took until the last week in June for the May invoices to be mailed. Once they were finally out the door, the notarizing of affidavits of performance and the preparation and mailing of invoices was made my responsibility. To prove that with proper focus and effort, it was not a daunting task, my wife and I worked through the Independence Day weekend to ensure that the June invoices were mailed on July 5.

Once the station had moved its studios and offices and its signal had been improved to cover the region, Jerry's next step in building WDVR's image as one of Philadelphia's major stations was to lease a fleet of Cadillacs for the salesmen and a couple of others to drive. Upon my return, the gold one was mine to drive! He wanted owner Dave Kurtz to drive one as well, but Dave would have no part of it; the best he would accept was a Ford station wagon.

No longer was WDVR to be looked upon as simply another of the several independent FM stations that had gone on the air in the Philadelphia region over the previous ten years. You must realize that, even by the late 1960s, WDVR was one of the few stand-alone FM stations anywhere in the nation that had achieved significant success.

When I returned to Philadelphia, I found the station in the midst of another move to position it in the big leagues radio-wise—a massive promotional endeavor called the $101,000 Sweepstakes (the station was located at 101.1 on the FM dial). People sent entries listing their Social Security number (who would do that today, with all the theft and fraud that's going on?). Each day, three entries were drawn and announced on the air several times throughout the day. If you heard your number announced and called in within something like ten minutes' time, you won $1,000. It also became one of my duties to deliver those checks. All these years later, I can still remember some of the places where the recipients lived. They were places I would not have wanted my family to live. It was a joy to hand them the check, as I knew those dollars would make a real difference in their lives, at least temporarily.

As a postscript to the WDVR portion of my radio life, let me note that on September 15, 1980, WDVR changed its call letters to WEAZ and started using the name EAZY 101. The station's TV promotions featured spokesman Patrick O'Neal telling viewers: "Other stations' call letters begin with a 'W.'

Ours begins with an 'E' for E-A-Z-Y." Of course, legally the station's call letters did begin with a 'W,' despite what O'Neal said on TV. When Easy Listening rival WWSH (106.1) switched to Top 40 in 1982, EAZY 101 was Philadelphia's only Beautiful Music station. During the mid-1980s and late 1980s, it was often tied for first place in the Arbitron ratings.

I share this because I would become associated with the station two more times in the twenty-year period following my departure in March of 1969. The first time was in the late 1970s, after we'd begun a programming and consultancy service for stations across the nation following our New York success, which you'll read about later. Within a few short years, we had become well established in providing stations with a successful musical format that was not dramatically different from what I had left the station with in 1969. In 1982, as part of the aforementioned competitor WWSH's change in format, we lost the station to our competitor, Schulke Radio Productions. However, my programming would once again return to EAZY 101 in the mid-1980s. (You'll see how some of this played out in Chapter 10.)

By late summer 1968, I felt I had delivered on what needed to be addressed and corrected when Jerry Lee originally asked me to return to WDVR, having quickly cleaned up the programming and internal office issues which had begun creating problems for the station, both ratings-wise and financially.

It was again time to seek another new challenge, to utilize the abilities I had been gifted with, but I wasn't sure where to look and whom to reach out to. I really had no desire to be a program director at another station, to serve under a manager who would challenge or simply not implement the range of elements that I knew were required to achieve the station's full potential. (WDVR was a unique operation from its very first day of broadcasting in May of 1963, as it still is more than fifty years later. Jerry is still at the helm and still functioning in a proactive mode, maximizing the station's assets in all areas of the operation, something too many in management never seem to learn.)

In the previous year, WDVR had achieved advertising revenues in excess of one million dollars; the first FM station ever to do so. It also had a solid audience ratings history, to which I had made a major contribution from its beginnings five years earlier. Putting this together with the personal experience I'd gained over the previous seven years, which had demanded a variety of talents and skills, I felt I could tell the owners of a struggling station, "I know how to lead your station to success."

The coalescing of all of these facts and combined experiences would be the seeds that would produce a move up the New Jersey Turnpike and into a coveted position as general manager of a New York City radio station—albeit an FM station with little audience.

WDVR was in the nation's number four market, plus we had conquered Boston, so it didn't seem sensible to look to a smaller city. I invoked a principle that I've always followed: when you're seeking action, whether it be in a small company, a large company, or a government agency, start at the top. In this case, I approached the top executives of companies owning stations that needed help and were located in the two top markets; Los Angeles and New York.

After reviewing Arbitron audience reports and choosing two stations in New York and one in Los Angeles, all of which had little, if any, audience, I prepared a to-the-point letter (I wish I still had a copy) observing that the station in question could use some help. I cited WDVR's ratings success and noted that it was the first FM in the nation to bill a million dollars in a year as a platform; I also described my role in it and, after a short review of my background, pointed out that I was confident I could lead their station to the same kind of success.

I cannot remember the station or owning company that I targeted in Los Angeles, but the two in New York were WN-BC-FM and WRFM, two of the poorest performers in the market, yet they possessed the two best FM signals with the least potential interference. WNBC-FM was of course owned by the National Broadcasting Company and, as I remember, didn't even appear in the ratings reports; WRFM was owned by Bonneville International Corporation, who had purchased it in 1966, and was number twenty-three out of the twenty-four stations included in the Arbitron reports at that time. (The 24th-ranked station was WHOM-FM, which I believe was still airing Chinese music.)

My letter regarding WRFM was sent to Arch L. Madsen, President of Bonneville, based in Salt Lake City, Utah. Only a short time passed before I received a call from Mr. Madsen; he was coming to the Freedoms Foundation headquarters, located adjacent to Valley Forge State Park northwest of Philadelphia to receive two awards. One on behalf of the Mormon Tabernacle Choir (Bonneville is the broadcast entity of the Church of Jesus Christ of Latter-Day Saints, also known as the Mormon Church) and the other for KSL-TV, Bonneville's TV station in Salt Lake City. He wanted to meet me and discuss my letter; he asked if it would be possible for me to pick him up at the Philadelphia Airport so we could talk as I drove him to Valley Forge. There was no hesitation on my part, of course!

I picked him up at the appointed time and transported him in style, as I was driving one of Jerry Lee's fleet of leased Cadillacs. Upon dropping him off at the Freedoms Foundation, Mr. Madsen said he felt good about our conversation and that I should expect to hear from Paul Bartlett, the present manager of WRFM, who would continue the discussion regarding my joining WRFM.

Paul Bartlett was an old-line broadcaster who had built KFRE-AM in Fresno, California, in 1942. He would go on to own it and its FM and TV counterparts, and he was a longtime friend of Mr. Madsen's. Paul was a true broadcast pioneer and had an interest in international shortwave broadcasting as well as American radio and television broadcasting.

Earlier in the 1960s, the Mormon Church had purchased a shortwave broadcast facility, WRUL, which had its beginnings in the 1920s as one of the world's first international shortwave stations. The story goes that the church fathers felt this facility could be a great proselytizing tool for the church to reach the peoples of other continents. However, once the purchase was approved, it was placed under the Bonneville umbrella and Mr. Madsen was expected to make it a profitable success through the sales of advertising, something that no shortwave station has ever achieved! While the station's studios were in New York, the transmitters—all five of them, transmitting with as much as 100,000 watts of power each—were located in Scituate, Massachusetts, on the Atlantic coast just south of Boston.

The station, with its enhanced programming and new call letters of WNYW—standing for "Radio New York World-wide"—did secure some business from multinational brands such as Coca-Cola, but this was nowhere near what was needed to sustain the operation. I need to note here that while this station is located and licensed in the United States, and in many cases can be heard throughout all or portions of the United States, it is not legally permitted to program or advertise to the residents of the continental United States. The purpose of shortwave is to reach people in other parts of the globe; in WNYW's case, the continents of South America and Africa were primary targets.

Along the way, someone came up with the idea that if the folks at the major New York advertising agencies could hear some of WNYW's programming, they'd recognize the opportunities the station offered for reaching the target customers in faraway lands. This is where WRFM came into the picture, as it had come on the market and could be the outlet for New Yorkers to hear WNYW. It was quickly acquired by Bonneville and had its signal upgraded to an antenna on the Empire State Building, from which most other New York City FM stations were transmitting. While this was a unique effort, it did little to generate new advertising for WNYW.

In 1968, after a series of management changes failed to produce meaningful results for either station, Paul Bartlett, having sold his stations, convinced Arch Madsen to allow him to see what he could do to grow WNYW into a successful venture. His efforts, unfortunately, produced no better results. At the same time, he did tackle the need for developing WRFM's programming in its own right, rather than continuing to duplicate WNYW's.

Being from California, Paul was aware of the Easy Listening programming being heard on KPOL (AM) in Los Angeles and the notable audience ratings success it was having. Using its musical structure as a guideline, he installed a similar format on WRFM. However, his content was not truly focused on what we'd learned the audience for this genre of music most desired, which had brought success to WDVR and WJIB. There were other factors as well: the station suffered from a lack of discipline in its non-music on-air content, and it was not able to have around-the-clock consistency due to specialty shows which aired at various times. In addition, New York already had a well-liked good music station, WPAT AM & FM, along with another station, WTFM, offering a half-decent lineup of music within the general realm. All these factors together meant that WRFM would not reap benefits from the changes Paul had made.

Hence, after a year of trying—and he'd come with a plan of not staying more than a year or so—and not succeeding, which was not his style, and with Arch Madsen back at Bonneville headquarters being under pressure to deliver positive results from his investment in the property, Paul Bartlett was ready to return to California and retirement.

It was not long after my on-the-road interview with Mr. Madsen (while most others called him "Arch," I had such respect for this man and what he stood for, in all of the eighteen years that I was affiliated with Bonneville, I could never bring myself to call him by his first name; at the most it was "Mr. M.") that I heard from Paul. He invited me to visit him at the station, located at 485 Madison Avenue—an historic address in radio history, as it had been the headquarters for the Columbia Broadcasting System (CBS) for more than thirty years, ending in 1964. Following the building's sale and completion of remodeling coming at almost exactly the time Bonneville acquired WNYW and, not long after that, WRFM, and as Mr. Madsen and his radio and TV stations were CBS affiliates, the lure of locating the stations' facilities at this address was too great to resist. (Prior to this time, WRFM's complete operation was located with its former AM sister station, WWRL, in the Woodside section of Queens.)

485 Madison Avenue – NYC

My arrival in Manhattan for that first meeting in December of 1968 found the city recovering from a recent snowstorm, with snow piled high along every street. The stations occupied an entire floor of the building, but my impression was that they were designed more with the shortwave operation in mind, with multiple studios looking in on the main WNYW control room. However, being a music person, I was impressed with the size of the record library and the quantity of LPs which it housed.

My session with Paul was quite cordial, with a great deal of time devoted to telling me of his extensive background (which I enjoyed hearing) and success and explaining in detail why he had the WRFM programming structured as it was. He believed it only a matter of time before the station would see success. The reason for hiring a new person to manage the station was not because it wasn't on the right track; rather, it was that he was ready to head back to California. We didn't come to any real agreement that day, but he sent me on my way with an understanding that we'd meet again early in the new year. I came away feeling good about our discussion, yet not quite as positive about the possibility of being hired as I had upon leaving Mr. Madsen.

Early in January 1969, I had a call from Mr. Madsen inquiring about how I felt about WRFM and working there. I stated that I still believed I could bring about the desired results which I had alluded to in my original letter. His reply was that he believed I was the right person for the position but that he wanted Paul Bartlett to reach that conclusion and make the decision, asking me to stay positive. By the end of January, I had been asked and did return to 485 Madison Avenue for what proved to be another cordial session. By its end, I had been offered and accepted the position of managing WRFM, which came with a significant increase in base compensation over what I was receiving in Philadelphia as well as a generous bonus plan tied to improved performance of the station, in both audience and advertising sales.

The position did not include any responsibilities for the WNYW shortwave operation, which would continue to operate from the same facilities. It was pretty much determined to be a lost cause, even though it continued to generate a few thousand dollars each month, mostly from a multi-hour block of Spanish-language programming involving one host and targeting residents of Central and South America. Of course, just the electric bill for operating four high-powered transmitters ate through multiple thousands of dollars per month.

What was likely to be the true highlight of my broadcasting career was about to unfold over the following two years. My employment agreement called for me to begin at WRFM at the end of March 1969, but it also stated that I would not officially become the manager until Paul's departure, which was scheduled for early July. During that intervening time, I would get acclimated to the operation and the staff, plan for any changes or improvements in programming and/or promotion and advertising, and consider ways for improving the sales operation; in addition, I would need to find a home in the New York metro area and get my family relocated. Meanwhile, I don't believe anyone in Philadelphia had an inkling about my planned departure, as I continued to fulfill all my duties.

The week before I was to begin in New York, the National Association of FM Broadcasters was holding its annual meeting in Washington, D.C. In that I was about to take on a rather high level and visible position in FM radio in the nation's number one market, I felt it made sense to attend this event. The most memorable part of the week—the only happening I really remember other than where it was held—was meeting up with Jack Masla, who headed a national radio advertising sales representative firm which represented WTFM, who would be our number two competitor, behind WPAT.

I don't remember whether it had been announced that I was joining WRFM or whether I told him. Regardless, when he inquired if I planned on airing programming similar to that at WDVR and I said "yes," he let out a giant laugh and advised me to stay in Philadelphia, as there was no way we would overcome the odds in New York.

CHAPTER 9

Taking the Nation's Number One Market: New York City

My arrival at WRFM at the end of March was a rather inauspicious happening, yet it was the beginning of a two-year period that turned out to be more exciting than I could have ever anticipated. I was super-charged and ready for action, but I wouldn't really be in charge until Paul Bartlett departed. I met all of the staff and began to settle in as we arranged a trade deal (services or merchandise in return for advertising on the station) for me to have a permanent room at the newly refurbished McAlpin Hotel, located across from Macy's and near the Empire State Building on 34th Street. Plus, I was provided a rental car for weekends so I could drive to my home in Pennsylvania, which I did on Friday afternoons, returning to New York either Sunday evening or very early on Monday morning. Both of these arrangements continued until we could purchase a home in Bergen County, New Jersey, and move the family.

I knew pretty much what needed to be changed and addressed in order to fulfill what I had assured Mr. Madsen several months earlier we could achieve in the nation's number one marketplace. I later learned that he was under the gun to show some degree of success for WRFM, as it had been three years since the station was acquired for $850,000, and, after several misfires and management changes, the church fathers were calling the acquisition a huge waste of money.

As I was a programmer who was bringing my successful format to the station, I was to be WRFM's program director as much as its manager. Hence, my first order of business was assembling my programming plans, so a great deal of my time was spent reviewing the list of in-play recordings and in the music library searching for other albums and selections we needed to get into play. This music library was quite large, filling several rows of shelves; it made the library we'd assembled at WDVR look like someone's small private collection.

However, I quickly learned that I had plenty of time to plan, as there weren't to be any visible—or should I say audible—changes made until Paul Bartlett had left the premises. I don't remember exactly what it was, but I made a minor adjustment in the overall sound, likely in the music mix. Whatever it was, it quickly caught Paul's ear and brought my first dressing down, in that when he said "no changes," that indeed meant nothing was to be changed until his watch had ended.

When I arrived at WRFM and began talking to people in the community, it quickly became evident there was definite confusion between the call letters WOR-FM and WRFM. Of course, the WOR call letters were legendary, as the AM station had a history dating to the early 1920s, and WRFM was hardly known. Our station ranked number twenty-three in the Arbitron rating reports, which, at the time, listed only twenty-four stations in the Big Apple. The only immediate way to address this from the station end was to have the announcers place an extra emphasis on the "R" when delivering the call letters.

What was quite different for me here was that, for the first time ever, I was walking into a fully staffed, fully functioning radio station. (Yes, I did join WBCN in Boston in a supposedly similar role, but it was such an increasingly chaotic situation, with Mitch Hastings constantly changing the game plan, no one was sure who was managing, if anyone was.) Hence, it was important for me to get to know the group of people I was inheriting. Rather than calling them one-by-one into my office, I visited them where they were. Even after our initial introductions, I made it a point of dropping by every office and the studios quite regularly. This included those that wouldn't normally be seen in a twenty-four-hour-a-day, seven-day-a-week operation. I would arrive in the city very early in the morning on occasion so as to see the all-night host, as well as go into the studios on the weekend to see part-timers who worked only those shifts.

I quickly discovered that this made several staffers very nervous and suspect of my motives. After realizing this, I probed to find out why, as I never played the "big, mean boss" role in any way. We were a team, and it would take every member's efforts to achieve the kind of win I was projecting. I was finally told that my predecessors (of which there were four or five in the three years that Bonneville had owned the station) all followed the same pattern of spending each day in their office—frequently behind closed doors—except for trips to the men's room and lunch. Many years later, management consultant and guru Tom Peters would identify the style of management/leadership which I used as MBWA, "management by walking around" or perhaps... "wandering around." While programming and our promotional campaigns were certainly keys to the station's success, this "down in the trenches" approach played a positive role as well.

After getting the musical product and plans in order, I turned to the marketing of our station after the changes were in place. Even though WRFM already had listeners and had been on the air since 1953, for many of our potential listeners, it generally was not a known entity and would be seen as a new station in the market. I had long planned for our initial method of promoting the station to be the FM dial card we'd used so successfully in Philadelphia, due to its low cost and the visibility and word of mouth it quickly generated. However, we needed a simple, easy-to-remember slogan or phrase that would attract attention. In addition to always calling ourselves WRFM Stereo 105 rather than just using the call letters, on the dial cards we chose initially to emphasize our key selling point, "Where the Difference Is the Music."

In each market where Bonneville owned one or more stations, they created a local board of advisors—made up mostly of prominent Mormons—that met quarterly with station management to discuss goals and the station's relationship with the community. During my first meeting with the group, having been in the position for only a few short weeks in what was the greatest opportunity in my broadcast career so far, I faced a challenge that required me to stand up for what I believed was right, putting my employment on the line. The chairman of the board suddenly made a declaration that he wanted to have the weekly half-hour Mormon Tabernacle Choir program aired three times each Sunday, not only in the morning but at 12:00 noon and 6:00 p.m. as well. I had to make a case on the spot as to why this would be an impediment to achieving the goals that we'd set for the station, as it would disrupt our utilitarian format of continuous music, which was to be the station's hallmark 166 hours a week. It wasn't that the Choir program was not a quality presentation, it simply would be a disruption during this vital weekend time period. As we had learned several years earlier at WDVR, daytime listening to stations playing this format was regularly higher on weekends than Monday through Friday.

After I diplomatically stood my ground by explaining that they likely had hired the wrong person, as doing this would hinder my fulfilling the promises I'd made to Mr. Madsen, the demand was rescinded. Another action that brought a dressing down by Paul Bartlett following the meeting was my response to a question asking what I saw as WRFM's financial future. I replied that I saw no reason it "shouldn't be throwing off at least $50,000 per month in profits by a year from now." Paul's opinion was that my statement was lunacy and I was committing hari-kari by giving the gentlemen such a number. (Paul would later write me a beautiful from-the-heart letter that both congratulated me and apologized for his actions. He really didn't see how we were going to bring the station the kind of success I was projecting. I'm not quite sure where it came from, but I had faith and an inner confidence we were going to make it happen.)

One of the kindest things Paul did for me before his departure was to take a necessary but unpopular action and to shoulder the resulting blame and anger rather than my having to deal with it; he terminated a nightly hour-long program called Music from Around the World, hosted by a gentleman named Erwin Frankel. The program was not bad, but it did not fit on the new WRFM, plus it was not an income generator for the station. Mr. Frankel did not go quietly, and he and his fans even purchased a full-page ad in the *New York Times* to protest and call for the station to lose its license, but no formal petition was ever filed.

Sometime in June, Paul announced that he'd be departing on July 3, so as to be home for the Independence Day weekend. So that became our D-Day—the day I'd been preparing for. Paul walked out the door for the last time on that morning, and the new format structure and music mix were instituted at noon.

As noted earlier, the sound WRFM was airing wasn't terrible musically, but it wasn't really in harmony with what (as I intuitively knew and as had been confirmed by my Philadelphia and Boston successes) the public was really hankering for; in addition, the lack of discipline on the part of the air staff was a major negative. The musical structure that proved so dramatically successful at WDVR and WJIB was 90% to 95% instrumental, and the one or two vocals that played in an hour were what you'd call "choral," in that they were groups of singers such as the Johnny Mann Singers and the Ray Conniff Singers. What WRFM's format did have that I decided had validity and made sense to keep were solo artist vocals, which have continued to be part of my programming approach to this day.

On air, in addition to the "Where the Difference Is the Music" slogan used on the dial cards, our prime liner was "All Music, All the Time." In this case, we played copycat, as "All News, All the Time" was the key promotional phrase used by the Westinghouse all-news stations, including WINS in New York.

When I arrived at 485 Madison Avenue, there were four musical hosts who divided their time between WRFM and WNYW. They covered 6:00 a.m. to midnight on WRFM along with a couple of hours each on WNYW, plus there were a couple of part-timers for weekends. A major change as related to these four gentlemen was that they would be going from being "gabby" hosts to warm, friendly staff announcers, with their prime voice duties being to identify the station once each quarter hour, announce the musical selections just played, and present a brief newscast every couple of hours.

As I was discussing this plan with each of them, one asked me whether, if after the ratings improved, they would be allowed to talk more. I had to tell him directly that no, this was not likely. At the same time, it was my plan to have three of them each fill a six-hour shift on WRFM, and a perfect position for the one who wanted to talk would be to handle the six or so hours of English language musical programming on WNYW they'd been sharing. This offer didn't sit well with him, as he'd not be heard in New York, so he chose to resign.

Having had the opportunity to fill in on the overnight shift at WABC Musicradio 77 on a couple of occasions, it was his hope he could become the permanent all-night DJ on the top-rated station. This did not come about, but the way was opened for him to capitalize on his warm, super-smooth announcer voice to become what is likely the most-heard-but-never-seen voice ever on American television, being heard more than ever today, nearly fifty years later. He introduces NBC's *Today* show each morning, is the voice of many awards shows, the Olympics, and other special events (such as the Memorial Day and July 4th patriotic performances from the U.S. Capitol on PBS), and was the commercial spokesman for Macy's for two decades. His name is Les Marshak.

Midnight to 6:00 a.m. was filled at the time with a semi-automated syndicated show featuring a female host using the name of Dolly Holiday, as the show was sponsored by Holiday Inns. I didn't have a problem with Dolly's voice and the show sponsorship; however, the music was totally out of sync with the rest of our programming. We might have been able to get away with leaving the show alone until the end of their contract, but I didn't feel it was worth the gamble. With a trip to corporate headquarters coming up, I chose to visit the advertising director at the Holiday Inns offices in Memphis on the way. I proposed keeping Dolly and the Holiday Inn commercials but using our regular programming. If that was not acceptable, then we'd need to cancel the show. The gentleman quickly smiled and declared he was happy to have it done our way.

As previously noted, with my background and knowing exactly how I wanted the station to sound, I acted as my own music and program director. One of the announcers functioned as the assistant program director, handling other details such as staffing and scheduling.

Other than music, we had to deal with a news and public

affairs commitment that was quite onerous for a musically oriented station. During the 1960s, the Federal Communications Commission was very aggressive in demanding stations commit significant amounts of time to these "community service" categories of programming and enforcing a station's fulfillment of their promises. This was particularly held over the heads of group owners, such as Bonneville, with the threat of their license renewals being challenged. Most stations fulfilled their requirements by burying an extended block of talk shows on Sunday mornings, beginning at 4:00 or 5:00 a.m. The folks at the FCC did not seem to be bothered by this approach; all that seemed to matter was that the promises and the delivery totals were equal.

I felt there had to be a better way to fulfill these obligations and be informative at the same time. First, we laid out a schedule of brief news summaries, which we'd air every half hour from 5:00 through 9:00 a.m. We aired them at fifty-seven minutes past rather than on the hour, so that we'd be back into music when most other stations were airing their news beginning at the top of the hour. Then, we aired them every two hours thereafter around the clock.

We had two newsmen on staff. During morning hours, this was great. Yet, the rest of the day, to have a newsman standing by to present a two-minute summary every two hours was a waste. Rather than lay him off, we redirected his efforts to inform-

Three members of the WRFM team in the early 1970's—Joe Roberts Caputo, Murray Roberts, and Mitch Lebe.
(Courtesy of Greg Katkowski collection)

ing listeners about events and organizations of note than didn't receive normal news coverage. Hence, Murray Roberts was appointed to the new position of Community Affairs Director. It was his job to find subjects that needed and deserved exposure and to create mini-reports about two minutes in length, usually in series form, that we'd air four times a day, at fifty-seven minutes past the hour in hours that did not have a newscast.

We also produced a special weekend feature named *Topic*, which aired vertically as a series of five reports every two hours throughout the day. One that Murray presented related to the City of New York spending an immense amount of money to purchase and remodel a large old home in a residential section of Brooklyn, designed as a halfway house for recovering addicts. Due to community pressure, it had sat for over two years without ever being opened. On the Monday following the weekend that this situation was exposed, in response to WRFM–a music radio station, not a news station, a TV station, or the famed *New York Times*–Mayor John Lindsay declared that the facility would immediately be opened.

Additionally, we'd read notable editorials from some of the region's many daily newspapers; and, each weekday evening at 7:57, the noted CBS network news commentator during World War II and years following, Quincy Howe, delivered a two-minute commentary on an event of the day. Granted, I might not had sought out Mr. Howe or anyone else to present such a report, but I had inherited him and certainly wasn't going to drop his daily news analyses as long as he desired to do them.

With all of these elements in place, we were fulfilling all of the burdensome obligations that our license carried except for one hour that aired on Sunday mornings between 7:00 and 8:00, following which was the one weekly broadcast of the Mormon Tabernacle Choir program. I don't remember what the actual content of the two half-hour programs was, but they were produced outside the station and dealt with issues that were relevant to our community and listenership, socially and artistically.

In reducing our Sunday morning block, one half-hour program that I cancelled was produced by the National Council of Churches. I didn't have any opposition to religion or the content of the program; it just was not a meaningful program for us to carry, especially since there was no evidence that anyone was listening. At the time of cancellation, I offered the organization a better substitute: have a group of local pastors record an ongoing series of sixty-second inspirational messages, which we would air at 6:00 a.m. each weekday morning and which would be heard by multiple thousands of individuals.

Since this required an effort greater than simply mailing us a tape each week, they protested loudly and filed a petition with the Federal Communications Commission. There were never any repercussions, either from the FCC or from listeners who missed the program. Regardless, we went forward with our sixty-second messages, rounding up a group of interested pastors from the metro area.

In view of all of the features and reports that we included in the daily schedule, I imagine you are thinking, "how dare they use the slogan 'All Music, All the Time'?" Well, the simple answer is that we still played more music per hour than virtually every other station in the market, AM or FM. Most carried more commercials than WRFM, and many had hourly newscasts longer than either our news or community affairs reports. Our prime format competitor, WPAT, had a full load of commercials and news, plus their music was badly in need of updating to be more appealing to the audience's changing tastes. Our other format competitor, WTFM, while more in tune musically, suffered from special program blocks, such as an hour of Broadway show music, along with an excess amount of chatter and a less-than-the-best signal.

As all of the on-air changes were being implemented during the first week of July 1969, it was time to get our "under the radar" audience-building campaign under way, to bring visibility to the station and its dial location and to generate word-of-mouth publicity.

Utilizing the cardboard holder Jerry Lee had designed in Philadelphia, which held about 125 cards, I harnessed the small team of college students that handled various projects for WNYW and sent them to the far corners of the metropolitan region, basically to any business within a fifty-mile radius of the Empire State Building that sold FM radios of any sort, to place a holder of our FM dial cards. As was the case in Philadelphia, business owners welcomed these postcard-sized cards, as they were useful for showing potential customers how many FM stations were now broadcasting. (Keep in mind, this was 1969 and FM receivers still were not universal items in homes and cars.) With the geographic shape of the New York metro area being what it is, I elected to produce three versions of the dial card. All three, of course, included the major New York City stations, with the main card including the few stations located north of the city. Then, there was a New Jersey edition, listing the suburban stations west of the Hudson, and a third one which included the Long Island FM stations. By October, more than a half million of the cards had been distributed through more than 2,000 locations.

WRFM Dial Card – front

WRFM Dial Card – back

Not thinking about budgets, I simply called the printer who'd been doing the station's printing work and told him what we needed and his shop began producing the cards and holders. As the bills began to arrive, Dick Grefe, our business manager, came to me to remind me that the station had no advertising budget. Since WRFM had been doing so poorly, and since its Los Angeles sister station had just spent more than $250,000 on an intensive campaign during the spring 1969 ratings period (after which the station's audience ratings went down), corporate management was not inclined to allow any real expenditures in New York. Dick's question was, "Where do we charge these?" Since this was printing, I replied, "Where else but office supplies?"

"We don't have enough money in that budget," was his reply.

"Let's just carry some over to next year," I said.

His response was, "We can't do that."

I'm not sure what he finally did, but my guess is that by the time this became a real issue, the station was showing enough signs of growth that we received a pass from corporate.

At this point, we did have a fair number of advertisers and commercials, but not so many that they came near to filling out the schedule, based on the seven-commercials-per-hour limit that I had instituted. An interesting aside: some listeners got the impression that we were actually a Brooklyn-based station, since quite a few of our advertisers were small businesses located in that borough. Why was this the case? The station's one sales person at that time, Jerry, lived there and this was easy territory for him to mine.

Shortly after becoming "captain of the ship," I was told that the station was sitting on more than $100,000 of advertising space that had been accumulated in *New York* magazine along with small print publications such as neighborhood weeklies and union newspapers. What was I to do with it? I couldn't let it go to waste, whatever its worth. We could do some generic ads, but we needed a "hook" to get people's attention. In surveying the broadcast schedules, I found we'd have no trouble clearing all commercials out

Music Bonus Hours

of one or two hours a day. So, we devised the WRFM Music Bonus Hours, later re-named the Total Music Hours.

We had our hook! We promoted these hours on air but never announced when they'd be scheduled, and we'd never slot them in the same hours two days in a row. Generally, one would air mid-morning to early afternoon and the other in the evening. It wasn't long before listeners began calling early in the day, inquiring as to which hours were scheduled that day.

Outside, they were promoted only in the publications that owed us advertising space. These fairly large ads read: "You get lots of music in every hour on Stereo 105... but look out for the WRFM Music Bonus Hours... where we play 59 minutes of music in an hour." Notice that there was never a mention of "no commercials." Commercials are a broadcaster's friend, and aired in every other hour in order to pay the bills. It wasn't long before this concept was being duplicated across many formats and cities. However, too many of the copycats made the mistake of talking about "commercial-free" hours.

While on the subject of advertising—The owner of the legendary Palisades Amusement Park, Irving Rosenthal, had an agreement with the privately owned Public Service Transport bus company (the forerunner of New Jersey Transit). The company operated bus routes throughout the New Jersey suburbs and into Manhattan, for the sales of advertising on the outsides of their fleet of buses. Mr. Rosenthal was always interested in trading his bus advertising space in return for commercial announcements on stations that he felt could help build the attendance at Palisades Park. Not many months after the station's transformation, WRFM's advertising began appearing on more than 600 buses in northern New Jersey. Hence, this became WRFM's first readily visible advertising. I considered the dial cards to be a "guerrilla"-style promotional campaign, where unlike billboards or newspaper or television ads, they were not readily visible to the general public.

By Labor Day, we felt it time to begin introducing the station to members of New York's large advertising community by placing a smallish box ad in ANNY, which stood for the *Advertising News of New York*, a magazine-style publication. However, it wasn't a typical ad; rather, it featured a mini-advice column titled "Dear gAbby," a take-off on the famous advice column of the day, where gAbby was asked a question to which "WRFM" was the logical answer. One of the early ads spoke of the dial cards and suggested that "if you have WRFM cards, you'll never end up playing solitaire." These ads were written by and carried a photo of the young lady––whose name, if I remember correctly, was Marion. She was our public relations and publicity director at the time.

Dear gAbby

GABIGAIL VAN LUREN

Dear gAbby: I'm a reasonably good looking account executive suddenly cut down at Christmas without one seasonal kiss from the "young things" in my agency. It's almost as if I had . . . bad breath! I know it can't be . . . we have four mouthwash accounts and two breath mints. I'm using our dandruff shampoo and I've just switched to our judo after shave . . . and still, no kisses! Is it this mistletoe shortage I read about? What do you suggest?   —No Yule Fuel
Dear No: Hundreds of business offices and other public places in the metropolitan area have found a new way to bring romance, happiness and friendliness back into the lives of their employees. They tune their FM radios to New York's most musical station, WRFM. Kissing has increased 37% since WRFM has come into so many lives. So . . . forget the mistletoe and try playing Stereo 105 throughout your agency. Every "young thing" in the office will soon be kissing you for it! By the way, for a special holiday, tell the girls about the 27-hour "Christmas Festival of Music" starting at 9 PM Christmas Eve!

Earlier, I mentioned the station being located at 485 Madison Avenue, which was the former headquarters for CBS–the

Columbia Broadcasting System. One day, while standing in the lobby waiting for someone, I looked up at the building's directory. Suddenly, a very familiar name jumped out at me, as having an office in Room 1300: *Mad* Magazine's one-and-only

Alfred E. Neuman! Keep in mind, this was an old building, and old buildings never had a 13th floor. Of course, Room 1300 would be on the 13th floor of the building. It was a clever bit of humor foisted upon visitors by the magazine, which at the time had its offices in the building... but not on the 13th floor.

Alfred E. Neuman © & ™ – E. C. Publications, Inc.

In the fall of 1969, most newspapers did not accept display advertising on their front page; however, the *New York Times* did sell one or two small classified-style listings that appeared at the very bottom of the front page. Once I noticed this, I could not resist taking part by placing the following message: "INVESTIGATION shows that WRFM's programming contains no artificial sweeteners. Only pure adult music is broadcast on FM Stereo 105." I don't remember that we received any particular reaction, but it was fun doing it.

As the placement of the dial cards in their holders continued throughout the fall, we never stopped seeking to refine the on-air product and ensure that our slogan, "Where the Difference Is the Music," was never in question in the listener's mind.

When the summer ratings report arrived in late September, we were not surprised to see no change in WRFM's ranking, as the survey period had begun before our on-air changes had been made and the dial card distribution gotten under way. At the same time, I wasn't quite prepared for the fall report, which arrived two days before Christmas. I can't say that in all of my eighty years have I received a more exciting Christmas gift than what was contained within the pages of the Arbitron listenership report: WRFM had moved from number twenty-three up to number ten, crashing into the big leagues of New York radio. We immediately became the talk of the Big Apple media and advertising communities. *Variety*, the show business newspaper, commented on the news and "found WRFM's unprecedented strength notable, since the station now outranks some well-known AM operations."

Meanwhile, sales reps for other stations who called on advertising agencies immediately went to work attempting to discredit our ratings success, proclaiming it was a total fluke. How could WRFM have amassed such a large audience in such a short period of time, experiencing such a big jump in only three months? These reps were also posing the question, "Where have you seen any advertising for them?" Of course, the answer was the 750,000 dial cards providing the vital information that WRFM was "New York's Most Musical Station," and the ecstasy that folks felt when tuning in; they just had to tell their friends what they'd found on their FM radio. The icing on the cake was the bus advertising in New Jersey, which I can't discount, as we were very strong audience-wise in the northeastern counties of the Garden State.

It didn't take long for advertising agencies to recognize the size of our daytime listenership, especially among women, and that WRFM was worthy of their clients' ad dollars. At the same time, our public relations and publicity lady departed and I replaced her with a gentleman who would a few years later become the station's and one of the market's most popular morning personalities, Jim Aylward. While Dear gAbby stopped giving advice to the advertising community, we saw it fitting that Aunt Martha should take up the mantle and provide valuable information about WRFM and its food-oriented advertisers to the

---

The Aunt Martha 1970 Very Big Market Report Column.*

by Aunt Martha

WRFM's
Merchandising Director,
Home Economist,
Food Shopper,
Consumer Affairs
Manager
and
general busybody.

Boys, I'm back again! Aunt Martha has just begun to write! And it looks like you have too.

AUNT MARTHA'S BAG:
Your cards and letters and notes on brown paper sacks have just been wonderful and I want you to know it. I'll try to answer some of your many questions on merchandising and the entire field of marketing of which I'm such an expert. I never told you but I've been in the business myself, you know. Oh yes. I ran Aunt Martha's Whip Shop in the Village, Cool Whip, Dream Whip. It was just a front for a supermarket but in the Village you have to do something!

Here's a question from Marvin L. who reads me all the time and wants to know what I think of Betty Furness' new appointment. Well, Marvin, I have to say it. Give credit where credit is due. I have never seen anybody open a door on a refrigerator any better, but my favorite actress is Wendy Barrie.

Here's one from all the cashiers at Key. They want to know what **Sacramento** tomato juice has in it that makes it taste so good and sell so fast. Well, I'll be honest, old Key friends, I don't know what they put in it. I can tell you what I put in it..which reminds me, think I'll whip up another Bloody Martha

now! Only kidding folks. But you know, **Sacramento** is honestly the best tomato juice I've ever tried. It has a tang and bite to it that is fresh picked perfection. I love it with lemon! And you should know that **Sacramento** is back again on another **WRFM** schedule of spots to help bring you more of those buying powerful Stereo 105 listeners. They'll do it too!

Now this one comes from a meat manager at Big Apple who asks what Aunt Martha knows about **Schickhaus** Quality Processed Meats (packaged and bulk). Well, I know **Schickhaus** is on the move bringing its quality since 1885 reputation to more people than ever before. And I know that in Nortn Jersey, **Schickhaus** Franks are the Number One seller..and they soon will be in your area too. **Schickhaus!** **Schickhaus** has brought its good name to **WRFM** and together they're telling those loyal listener-shoppers the facts of franks; the frank facts of franks..now, they've got Aunt Marthaus doing it!

This question is from the merchandising director of another radio station. He

wants to know how come I know so much about marketing. Well, I owe it all to a long and wonderful life, an intense interest in food and from reading _his_ columns.

This last note from Charlie, Assistant Manager, says, "Aunt Martha, how can I get to be Manager. I'm sick of assisting!" Charlie, the answer is Accent. It wakes up flavor that nature puts in food. And now that **WRFM** is accenting **Accents'** message to wake up New York area shoppers, you can really make a Manager out of yourself quickly. All you do is accent the **Accent**. Those **WRFM** listeners will be on the lookout for it. And, Charlie, if you feature products advertised on **WRFM** you'll be a Manager in _my_ book and I'll be _your_ assistant!

Until the next one's spun..so long, have fun and goodbye out there!

(For an answer to your questions on merchandising write Aunt Martha, WRFM, 485 Madison Ave., N.Y., N.Y. 10022)

*Aunt Martha's column is written under the influence of Postum.

Aunt Martha column

---

immense metro area food industry via its monthly _Modern Grocer_ publication. As you see, these were written in the serious, yet tongue-in-cheek style, as only Jim could write.

With the station moving into the upper ranks among New York's many stations in listenership, it was time to beef up our sales force; as noted, we had only one salesperson, and he focused primarily on selling to individual shopkeepers. As I discussed the matter with the holders of the purse strings at corporate headquarters, they were not prepared to commit many dollars toward building the strong team that would maximize the return which our ratings potentially offered. We finally were able to employ a sales manager who had been with WPAT in the past, plus two sales representatives who'd had a small amount of media sales experience.

In most major cities, especially New York, radio stations handled all business coming from advertising agencies, regardless of whether the advertiser was a national business or one serving just the metropolitan area. Their national advertising representative firms solicited business only from outside the station's service area. In our case, I chose to allow our national representative—Alan Torbet Associates—to cover all of the large New York City advertising agencies, which placed the bulk of all advertising buys for national advertisers, on our behalf, as we simply did not have the manpower to do the job. (Regardless of the limitations and a slow start to the year, we'd end 1970 with nearly a million dollars in advertising revenue, and the 1971 number was destined to be much higher.)

Along about this time, business manager Dick Grefe, who was responsible for the WNYW shortwave operation—as I was hired to manage only WRFM—came to me bemoaning the cost of operating the station, considering there was virtually no revenue nor much potential for any. Keep in mind, paying the electric bill for the operation of five high-powered transmitters was painful in itself. We put our heads together and devised a plan to save several thousands of dollars per month by shutting down studio operations in New York and the costly telephone lines connecting to Scituate, Massachusetts. Instead, we'd have each of the WRFM hosts record a series of fifty-five-minute DJ shows on tape, which would be sent along with a couple of tape decks up to the transmitter facility, and the engineers there—who could not be eliminated—would become studio operators as well. The station already aired the CBS network top-of-the-hour news summaries, and henceforth they'd simply be fed directly into Scituate rather than through our New York studios. Why not save money by simply shutting the station down? Corporate management had made the decision that was not an option, but they began seeking a buyer, and it was eventually sold.

By early spring 1970, the winter ratings report had arrived, finding WRFM firmly entrenched in the top five among all stations. We had continued our FM dial card promotion, with more than one million cards having been distributed by the time this survey period was under way. The cards continued to build awareness and keep word-of-mouth flowing, plus we'd begun using posters in some train and bus stations, followed a little later by lighted signs along the tops of New York City buses. At the same time, we'd taken up a new slogan for our dial cards and other advertising: "Begin to Like Radio Again." As you'll note, all of our promotional slogans carried

Our first poster ad, placed in selected rail and bus stations in the metropolitan area.

WRFM NYC Bus Top

an underlying message: there's something out of the ordinary about this radio station and its programming.

Relative to the audience ratings, I found that WRFM's rise to the upper ranks among all stations did not tremendously impact the audiences of our two in-format competitors, WPAT-AM & FM and WTFM; we simply surpassed them. The station which experienced the greatest drop in their ratings at the same time we were growing was an AM station, WNEW. It's my sense that our dial cards, which engendered great word-of-mouth about WRFM and our more familiar and mass-appeal variation of the Easy Listening/conservative popular music format, caused a great number of folks to transition to the FM band, perhaps for the first time. Another factor was that by the late 1960s, this legendary station, which had been a mainstay for tens of thousands of New York radio listeners for decades, with its music and personalities format dating back to the 1930s, was losing its way and leaving its heritage programming—and its devoted listenership—behind. Since my earliest days of programming, it's been my theory that once a station locks in a listener, losing that listener would be a matter of that station causing the listener to leave rather than a competitor stealing him or her. Also, I believe that our "Begin to Like Radio Again" slogan had truly resonated with these folks.

A side story that demonstrates the popularity to which WRFM had risen by the summer of 1970: we had purchased season tickets to the great summer entertainment venue located in the northern New Jersey coastal area, the Garden State Arts Center. One of the performances was by Steve Lawrence and Eydie Gormé. At one point during the concert, they asked the audience for requests. Because we were sitting in the fourth or fifth row, it was easy to be heard. I called out a request for Eydie to sing "Hallelujah," a song which I liked but which was hardly known by the masses, as it was released only as a 45-rpm single, which got scant attention.

Eydie immediately responded, "How do you know about that song?"

I said, "I play it on WRFM."

She repeated "WRFM," and the whole place erupted in applause.

Come summer, when the spring ratings report was released, we experienced some slippage, dropping down a few positions in the rankings. Of course, the other stations whose ad sales depended on ratings immediately pounced on our drop with a unison response, "See, their ratings success was a fluke!" However, we at the station had not sensed any lack of enthusiasm on the part of the listeners; we'd continued our dial card program and had added signs above the doors and windows in the New York City subway cars. Throughout this period, even if it hadn't been said in so many words, we played up the message that WRFM was "radio designed for you, the listener."

Something I learned working with Jerry Lee in Philadelphia was to always stay on the offensive! Not knowing what the summer ratings would show, we took action. In New York City, a lot of people from all walks of life ride the subway, as it's really the best way to get around. At the end of every subway car was a position for a square ad measuring something like 15 by 15 inches. We purchased this space in every subway car of every subway line in the system for thirty days, coinciding with the approach of the fall audience survey period. The ad design contained a lot of white space with our call letters in giant print right in the middle, followed by this message: "Why the big letters? Because that's our name and we're the biggest name in adult music radio. That's why. We're the one you listen to." Of course, this action proved unnecessary, as the summer report positioned us right back in the top five of all stations. However, we didn't want to gamble on a second ratings report showing decreased listenership, or miss an opportunity to grow our audience even more.

After completion of the run of the big call letter ads, we returned to the side panel signs in the subways, utilizing the same basic message used in earlier posters but with a portion carrying a new slogan, "The Radio Pollution Fight-

ers," and a photo of five very stern faces belonging to staff members. The thinking behind this headline was that radio in general was becoming more and more loaded with advertising and fewer and fewer stations were playing music that was appealing to the huge segment of the population that we were reaching.

By the latter part of 1970, it was time to produce a brochure for distribution to advertising agencies and major advertisers which told our story. We included our histo-

ry and programming philosophy, advertising campaigns, our impressive list of advertisers, and excerpts from some letters from listeners. The cover of the multi-page folder simply said, "The Story of WRFM. A radio broadcasting tradition since 1969." That last statement was a quirky play off of those who make big, bold claims about their history or greatness; this brochure was distributed in 1970, proclaiming our tradition to be a full year in length!

Our FM dial cards had become an extremely popular item and had done such a spectacular job in spreading the word about the station that I got another idea. While walking through Bloomingdale's department store one eve-

ning in early fall 1970, I spotted a pedestal tea cup decorated with Grecian figurines. Brainstorm: What if we could find who imported this cup and have the figurines replaced with a wrap-around of our dial card to use as a promotional tool to the advertising community? We did succeed in locating the importer, who reported that the factory in Japan certainly could fulfill our request, but we'd need to order a couple of thousand pieces and there'd be a four-month lead time.

Along with my typical impatience in such matters, a nervous concern was whether during that time someone would file for a call letter change. Yes, they would; midway through the wait, the American Broadcasting Company decided their FM stations should have their own call letters. However, we were saved by two factors. First, call letter changes were not simple, overnight deals like they are today. Second, ABC proposed to change WABC-FM in New York to WRIF, another set of call letters including both an "R" and an "F." As soon as the announcement appeared, I was on the phone to our Washington attorney, asking him to protest the requested call letters as ones that would further confuse listeners. The FCC agreed, ABC simply swapped WRIF with their requested calls for Detroit, WPLJ, and the whole process took long enough for us to get our cups in hand and out to the advertising community!

Carrying out a concept or action in an unorthodox manner always intrigued me, especially if it would put our call letters in front of a large number of eyeballs at a reasonable price. About this time, artist Robert Indiana's LOVE sculpture

was becoming famous and was even placed on a postage stamp. I got the idea of adopting this design (poor Mr. Indiana had never trademarked or copyrighted his great piece of work, so he never earned a cent from it beyond some publicity) for printing WRFM's call letters on our stationery in this design. Not long afterward, a young entrepreneur showed up, offering us a large flat space on the side of a building that he'd just obtained the billboard rights for. I couldn't resist, and very soon the WRFM call letters, LOVE style, with "stereo 105" just below were painted on this wall, to be seen by drivers heading south on New York City's Major Deegan Expressway. We did get a few complaints from residents of the area, claiming we were degrading their neighborhood. Thinking back to that time, they could have had a much uglier ad up there instead of our beautiful, colorful call letters.

As the end of 1970 approached, we were invited to originate a daily broadcast from the International High Fidelity Showcase, a permanent trade show and exhibit which had opened in lower Manhattan earlier in the year. A music station with limited talk, did this make sense? No station in the Easy Listening genre had ever done it; yet, we were a highly rated station with a definite emphasis on quality in our technical sound. I said, "Let's go!" This would be a complete studio setup, virtually replicating our studio at 485 Madison. While it was impossible for us to have every listener visit the station and see the operation in

Ken Lamb at the Showcase
(Courtesy of Greg Katkowski collection)

person, they'd now be able to see popular WRFM host Ken Lamb doing his actual live broadcast for two hours each afternoon, five days a week, playing the musical recordings and commercials and announcing song titles and artists of the music just played, just the same as in the studio.

As the year was coming to a close, the fall 1970 Arbitron audience report showed—to the surprise and chagrin of many in New York radio—that WRFM was number two in the market, directly behind either WABC or WOR. They were the two powerhouse AM stations of the time, but at this point I cannot remember which one had the lead. The longtime high-ranking Easy Listening stations, WPAT-AM & FM, had been surpassed back when we moved into fifth place.

The last major advertising effort we did before I gave up managing the station to devote my full efforts to our new programming and consultancy service was a full-page ad in the *New York Times* on Tuesday, January 26, 1971. We affectionately called this the "teacup ad," as it pictured a cup upright at the top and turned over at the bottom, signaling full and empty. It featured an extremely bold headline which read, "THE 24 HR WRFM BREAK" and listed every song, by title and artist, that we'd be playing for the 24-hour period beginning at 6:00 that morning through 6:00 the following morning.

Many might describe our approaches to promoting and advertising the station, both to potential listeners and to advertisers, as unorthodox and thinking "outside the box," which has become a popular phrase in more recent years. Some might well call them "guerrilla tactics," as most of our activities were unexpected and not likely to be anticipated. Things like the dial cards and the newspaper ad listing a full day's musical programming had been done in Philadelphia but, to the best of my knowledge, never before in New York. The placement of more than two million FM dial cards in several thousand locations was far too labor-intensive for most managers to even consider. In addition, I came up with tongue-in-cheek-like phrases, such as "Begin to Like Radio Again" and "The Radio Pollution Fighters," in the hope of capturing people's attention and prompting them to action.

We may have recognized this in Philadelphia and/or Boston, but I came to a full realization of the fact that this format and genre of music attracted a broad range of ages and spanned the full socioeconomic spectrum, from taxicab drivers to bank executives. Over the years, we've heard from hundreds, perhaps thousands, who told us that "the station," while perhaps not their favorite programming, was their choice when driving, especially during commuting time, in order to reduce the stress and keep their blood pressure in check.

It was a thrill to conquer the nation's number one metropolitan area, and this period certainly proved to be one of the two or three most exciting times in my working life. Looking back, I realize that when I went to New York in 1969, there was no question in my mind that we would succeed; if anything, the success came faster than expected. I never expressed this to anyone: we molded a great team of individuals, 80% of whom I inherited, into a pro-active force committed to excellence and winning. I just don't think any one of us realized how ready the market was for what we had to offer.

I had very mixed emotions in stepping away from WRFM;

it was like giving up my baby. However, to fulfill Mr. Madsen's wishes, it was time to take on another new challenge, changing my focus from one city to seeing the entire nation as my "community."

CHAPTER 10
Syndication Years

After WRFM's success, Bonneville International Corporation President Arch Madsen had called to say that he wanted our programming on Bonneville's other six FM stations as soon as we could provide it. At the same time, if we were gearing up to serve six stations (seven counting WRFM), why not offer our services to stations in areas not reached by any of the Bonneville stations? I proposed that to Mr. Madsen, and he said, "Go!" And that's how my music began being heard all over the United States, through a process known as syndication.

Syndication works much differently than regular radio. In a network, such as NBC or CBS, the affiliates all pretty much air the programs or shows at the same time, usually receiving the programming by telephone line—now via satellite—at the time of broadcast. In syndication, the producer packages the program or format and provides it to subscribing stations by some electronic means for airing by the individual station at an appropriate time.

The format and musical formula that began in Philadelphia in 1963 and continued four years later in Boston paved the way and provided the knowledge and insights needed to achieve what occurred in the nation's number one market. The next evolutionary step consisted of packaging our music, which up to this time was played directly from LPs one track at a time, onto reels of stereo tape. It was more than time that we made this transition, as this was the only logical way to deliver the music and control how it played on each individual station.

While it would require additional manpower to handle the mechanics, it wouldn't be highly difficult to provide the client stations with our programming. Beyond a library of reels of tape totaling well over two hundred hours of programming, we'd provide daily schedules of exactly what tape to play at what time, as well as providing them with detailed written instructions for executing the format plus guidance for promoting and advertising their station. Still, we wouldn't be there to hold their hand or directly provide the motivational energy which was key to WRFM's success. That was to be the real challenge!

We were well into 1970 at this point, and our first challenge was to get a library of Christmas season music segments produced to get Bonneville's newly acquired Chicago FM station, WCLR, on the air in December of 1970. Initially, we were operating in the middle of WRFM's facilities, which was not going to be practical long term, but that would be dealt with later as the deadline approached.

Serving multiple stations required us to acquire high-quality tape recorders and other equipment and to bring on qualified individuals to record the master tapes, from which copies would be made and shipped to client stations by another division of Bonneville International. At the beginning, we were simply called WRFM Program Services, as all of this was developing while I was still managing the radio station.

By this time, it had been decided that we would set up a division separate from WRFM within the Bonneville corporate family and that I would leave WRFM management and concentrate on developing our programming syndication and consultancy services.

Early in 1971 we hired Loring Fisher, who had a technical background and was in sales for broadcast equipment manufacturer Gates Radio Company, to be our number two person, responsible for sales and administration. Not long after this, we extracted our new programming syndication operation from the middle of the radio station, moving to space on another floor of 485 Madison Avenue, and re-naming the new separate entity Bonneville Program Services.

BBC Vice President Loring Fisher and Director of Operations Walter Powers. (Courtesy Greg Katkowski collection)

Later, we changed our name to Bonneville Broadcast Consultants. This name was more appropriate, as we realized that most stations needed not only a professionally programmed and competitive programming package to fill the airwaves. Also, in many cases, they required guidance in promoting and advertising their product as well as assistance in fine-tuning their technical facility. A factor we always needed to keep in mind was that many of our client stations would be automated operations, meaning that there was not an announcer on duty specifically to handle the playing of the tapes; a machine would be running the station. Tapes would be changed and the automation system minded by a person whose primary responsibility was manning the sister AM station.

If the term "automation system" is not familiar to you, let me explain. Today, a radio station programming automation system (meaning there's no need for hands-on human involvement) is easily contained on the hard drive of a computer. In the 1970s it was a different story—automation systems were electromechanical in design, occupying two or more large equipment racks. As noted, musical programming would originate

This is what a basic automation system from mid-20th century era looked like (Courtesy Chuck Conrad, Chalk Hill Educational Media, Inc.)

from reels of stereo tape and all announcements, whether station ID's or commercials, would each be on an NAB (National Association of Broadcasters, which set the standards) endless-loop cartridge. Therefore, a system would be equipped with four or more reel-to-reel tape decks, each capable of playing reels at least 10-1/2" in diameter, along with two or more carousel or tray-style players—each holding thirty or so cartridges—from which the non-music elements aired. At the end of each musical segment or selection we inserted a sub-audible tone, with the same being done for each announcement as well... hence triggering the start of the next element, based on what had been programmed into the system's controller.

As we rolled through the first half of 1971, among our early outside clients were the Malrite Broadcasting FM stations in Milwaukee, Rochester, New York, and Minneapolis-St. Paul. Of the three, Rochester's WEZO had a dramatic story to tell, rapidly gaining a huge audience, which it would retain for many years to come. At times, it commanded 20% of all listening in the Rochester market. Another early client was KMEO in Phoenix which, by the fall 1971 survey period, had also achieved great success and, like WRFM in New York, moved ahead of long-time Good Music-formatted KRFM. I do not remember or have records of the chronology of our other client stations, but we were beginning to build an enviable track record in cities across the nation.

In July of 1971, I personally traveled to Los Angeles to spend two weeks getting Bonneville-owned KBIG-FM up and running and its product refined. I'm not quite sure where to begin with the saga of KBIG. Here was the most powerful FM station in Southern California with by far the best coverage of just about any major-market FM in America. However, it lived within an operation that suffered the worst misallocation of assets I've ever seen. This mighty FM station was being "staffed"– but totally unattended–by the largest radio station automation system I've ever seen. Meanwhile, its 10,000-watt AM daytime sister, licensed to and transmitting from Avalon on Catalina Island, received all of the attention provided by a full staff, including a crew of major-market-caliber air personalities. Neither station achieved any significant ratings, and most of the duo's revenues–which were miniscule–were generated by the AM station airing special events, such as the Baja California road races.

I finally concluded that such a large automation system had been installed so that it would require attention no more than about once a day, unless there was a breakdown... which occurred quite frequently. Prior to my arrival, the FM programming was being provided by a third-rate (read "cheap") music service.

Our first priority was to get the automation system modified to play our Bonneville tapes, which were seven-inch reels, each containing two quarter-hour segments, and to change the voiced station identifying messages. Next was to have the air staff members begin recording current news and weather reports– which they had not been doing–on our schedule of once every three hours and more frequently during early morning hours.

Our next challenge was for the general manager to realize that the future was with the FM station and to quickly minimize the man-hours committed to the AM station. Even the program director wasn't quite ready to get on board. By the time I left, we had the station sounding pretty good and competitive, even though it was still fully automated. However, we did have the air staff fulfilling the schedule of weathercasts and news reports.

As for weather reports, someone reminded me recently that I had coined the term (at least as far as radio and TV were concerned) "Southland" to describe the vast Los Angeles region, which stretched from mountains and desert on the north and east to the Pacific Ocean on the west. My thinking was that with the differences in the weather across the region, at least in temperatures, giving a detailed report was too time-consuming... so we went with a brief "consolidated" forecast under the "Southland" heading, which seemed to satisfy everyone.

After returning to New York, I conceived the idea of convincing the existing general manager to take on one of my New York staffers, Fred Seiden, as his new program director, on a six-month trial basis. Fred was extremely detail-oriented, knew how to talk to air personalities, and fully comprehended what made WRFM so successful!

It boded well for everyone that, before too many months passed, the general manager retired and was replaced by Joe Dorton, who had been the manager of WCLR when it was launched several months earlier. Fred and Joe—both of whom left this earth much too young—were a perfect duo. They were go-getters committed to success and excellence, Joe working in sales and promotion and Fred being fiercely protective of the on-air product. When Joe or a salesperson would show up with some concept that Fred felt would negatively impact KBIG's programming sound or image, he'd fight it all the way. That's how you become a station that's highly successful while making the listener the number one priority.

It didn't take long for the station to become a major force in southern California radio—and remain one for many years. Looking at the audience ratings reports for the spring of 1978, KBIG was the number two most-listened-to station in greater Los Angeles, and to the south in Orange County, it ranked number one with nearly ten percent of the radio listening. An example of the love felt for the station is just a few lines from a long letter to the editor printed in the Monday, April 24, 1978 issue of the *Bulletin* in Anaheim, California. It was from Mrs. Regina Seeley, in which she wrote: "Give your big color TV to Uncle Herman... throw away your *TV Guide*... renovate your old stereo, or better, buy a new one. Turn your set to FM 104, KBIG. Leave it there. Settle back to perpetual enjoyment."

While the programming product was right on target, we had realized along about a year or so before that the technical aspect of what we were delivering really needed an upgrade in quality. The decision was made to construct an entirely new library from scratch. At the same time, the seven-inch reels of tape, which held only a half-hour of programming in two quarter-hour segments, was proving to be a logistical nuisance to many of the stations. Therefore, we turned to 10½-inch reels, which held a full hour's worth of programming, playing at 7½ inches per second.

To ensure top quality in sound, each musical selection would be mastered on tape at fifteen inches per second, which better permitted the editing out of clicks and pops that are inherent in pressed recordings. I've always been amazed that these flaws

Greg Katkowski was a key person in our tape mastering operation—he's seen here in our Tenafly recording studio.

can be cut out of the tape without there being any negative impact or "burp" in the musical performance.

Since our recording engineers had their hands full extracting the best sound possible from the original recordings and, in some cases, adjusting the equalization within the audio spectrum (such as bass vs. treble) to provide the most pleasant listening experience when transmitted by an FM station, we hired a young lady named Minerva to handle the "de-popping" function. I don't remember what her background or experience was, but we quickly dubbed her "the fastest razor blade in the East." She proved fast and truly adept at her job, which involved sitting in a room with a large tape deck and headphones, with a razor blade in hand for precision cutting of the tape and splicing tape for putting it back together minus the "pop." A lot of work, a lot of detail... but our stations henceforth were to have a flawless product, giving them sound quality that was unequaled.

One of our earlier major success stories was in Cleveland, where, similar to New York City and WRFM, we were taking on a long-time, well-entrenched competitor. Our new client there, WQAL, was owned by SJR Communications, headed by one Edward Cossman. Their offices and ours were just blocks apart in New York City, so Eddie came over to sign the contract and press me for exactly how we planned to achieve success for their station. My only response was to say "trust me, I'm not prepared to reveal our strategy yet." This was an honest answer as, while I had some concepts in mind, it required that I do some monitoring of a couple of other Cleveland stations after we arrived in the market to set things up, lay out the format guidelines, and train the staff in carrying them out.

Our Cleveland competitor was WDOK, an old-line Good Music station that had its beginnings on AM, like WPAT in the New York market, before adding an FM counterpart. I had two questions in mind that, while many might consider to matter little, I felt provided information needed for us to use in identifying WQAL in such a way as to sink into the listener's subconscious to the extent that they'd not forget the station's name or dial position.

The owners were not about to change WQAL's call letters, so that became a given. Then, what options are there for differentiating your new station from your prime competitor who is well entrenched in the marketplace with very familiar call letters and dial location? In the market, there was one other station with a "Q" in their call letters, WABQ, an AM station. Question one was, did they emphasize the "Q" in any way; the answer was that they did not. WDOK-FM was at 102 on the dial, WQAL not far away at 104. WDOK always identified themselves as 102 FM, that being the second bit of information I needed. So, WQAL instantly became "Q104," carrying enough impact to give us a leg up. When it utilized our programming, and didn't vary from our instructions for executing the format, WQAL followed WRFM's lead and before many months passed, surpassed its high-rated competitor in the audience ratings.

I believe it was in 1972 that WQAL came on board. Fourteen years later in 1986, the station was still a dominant force in Cleveland radio, ranking number two among all radio listeners, and during many of the intervening years, it held the number one position.

Since a fair number of our client stations would be automated, and because this was a music-intensive format with little talk, I felt it important that the stations recognize holidays— so the audience would know that there was someone at their station who knew what day it was. To accomplish this, we began producing a special message of about one minute in length for each significant holiday of the year, which the stations could air several times through the day.

Of course, our music service not only included a full library of tapes for the Christmas/ winter holiday season but also had reels of music specifically for the patriotic holidays as well as St. Patrick's Day, Thanksgiving, and others. And, from time to time, we produced specials for our stations to air, such as one for a Valentine's Day in the 1970s when Johnny Mathis did

MRT & Johnny
Mathis

the hosting honors. We recorded it in the KBIG studios on Sunset Boulevard in Hollywood not far from Johnny's home, with yours truly producing.

By no means was WQAL our only success story; by the 1980s, we had more than 150 stations utilizing our programming, including 6KY, located "down under" in Perth, Australia (the "6" at the beginning of its call sign indicates it is located in the state of Western Australia). Taking on an Australian client placed an extra demand on us in the programming area, as Australia had enacted a law similar to Canada's, requiring a certain percentage of music played on each radio station to feature an Australian artist. Lightening the burden a little in providing this material for 6KY was that we were already playing several songs by singer Olivia Newton-John plus selections by a pianist named Bruce Rowland and Sydney's Festival Strings, which were releasing orchestral recordings of popular melodies. Also, we discovered a singer named Kamahl, who at the

Our one-and-only station "down under" in Perth, Australia.

time was one of the country's most popular vocalists and fit perfectly within our format, so much so that we began including him in our regular programming from time to time.

Throughout these years, many of our stations in large and medium-size cities across the nation could be found among the top four or five stations, both FM and AM, in the Arbitron ratings, even though they were playing what some, especially sales reps for competing stations, called "elevator" or "dentist office" music. However, the ratings were not lying: hundreds of thousands were listening and enjoying this music, which featured instrumental arrangements of melodies they grew up with, hour after hour and day after day.

Not long after our Cleveland success, the manager there transferred to the sister station in Washington, and we were quickly asked to program it as well. From several aspects, the challenges in the nation's capital were greater. First, the prime competitor, WGAY (FM), was better programmed, having taken my counsel to heart when I advised them just a few years earlier prior to our launching the syndication entity, and had more astute management. Plus, the manager, who had listened and responded to all of our advice in Cleveland, suddenly had all his own answers in Washington. Still, WJMD did achieve a modicum of success and even made it into the top five stations ratings-wise on more than one occasion over the next few years during which they utilized our services.

Another early client was WHOM ("We're High On the Mountain," meaning New Hampshire's Mount Washington), call letters that had been in use for many years in greater New York City, where Norm Alpert, the new owner of the FM was from; he had purchased it in 1972 when its TV sister station owner decided to dispose of the radio side. With the transmitter on the top of Mount Washington, the station could be heard over much of the northern half of New England. It was difficult to go most anywhere north of Boston and mention "WHOM Radio" without someone saying, "that's the Mount Washington station."

At least once a month, I'd receive a call from the general manager of our client in one of the larger Midwestern markets who would immediately launch into a detailed review of all that was going on radio-wise in his city. From an industry perspective, it was at times interesting, yet most of the stations discussed and their target audiences had no relevance to or impact on his station's success or failure. Yet, his station did not rank as high in the ratings as it could have. After a few minutes, I'd break in and ask about his own station, about which he'd have little to say. Then I'd have to be as diplomatic as possible and bring up the multiple items that I knew needed attention. They were known issues, as one of our requirements for our larger market clients was to have a telephone number which was tied directly to their live broadcast signal, which gave us the ability to dial up and listen at any time. Yes, we did monitor these stations on a regular basis.

This manager must have been the motivation or inspiration for my writing an article published in *The Pulse of Broadcasting* sometime during the 1980s, which was headlined, "Who's Tending the Store, Or Who's Leading the Parade, Or How's Your Mirror Image?" (You'll find it reprinted in the Appendix of this book.)

Come 1974, with myself and my two key associates, Loring Fisher and Frank Murphy, all living in Bergen County, New Jersey, it seemed to make sense that we move our operation out of Manhattan. This would reduce the burden of commuting into the city every day, especially when we seldom had station personnel visit our offices. Rather, we went to visit their facilities. Plus, we would be able to have more space without increasing costs, and personally, we'd escape the onerous New York state and city income taxes.

For many years, Frank Murphy was the leader of our client station support team. (Courtesy Greg Katkowski collection)

While a couple of our staffers chose not to come along to the suburbs, one who did was our recording engineer, Greg Katkowski. We had gotten to know Greg when he started showing up for Len Lamb's daily WRFM remote broadcast from the International High Fidelity Showcase. Ken trained Greg in running the controls and playing the recordings, giving Ken more time to chat with the many visitors who stopped by. Greg was a good learner, making him a perfect candidate when we needed someone for this very meticulous and detail-oriented work. (Writing this takes me back to when in 1955, I began regular visits to a little radio station in Trenton, New Jersey... leading to my first paying job in radio.)

Somewhere along the way, from our monitoring sessions and in-market visits, we observed that any number of the on-air folks at the stations, while being very competent, failed to put a smile in their voice when talking on the air. It was the mid-1970s and the "smile button" craze had just hit. This inspired me to buy a batch of these buttons and send a couple to each of our client stations, to be clipped onto the holders of the microphones into which these individuals talked—hopefully to be a reminder.

A *Track Record* report covering the Arbitron audience survey period of April–May 1978 listed forty-seven client stations which ranked number five or higher in total week averages for adults aged eighteen years or over, many within the top three positions. These stations were in locations from Albany, New York, to Winston-Salem, North Carolina, with many major markets such as Houston, Detroit, Los Angeles, and Denver included as well.

At this point, the BBC division had not yet reached its peak in the number of client stations and success. Our prime competitor within the genre was Schulke Radio Productions and their stations, the majority of which were in larger markets. As our expertise and support helped station managements

who were committed to winning in markets such as Dallas-Fort Worth (KMEZ) overcome the Schulke-programmed stations in the ratings, it became easier to secure additional clients, especially ones with better technical facilities and good management.

In 1963, the era in which WDVR Philadelphia was launched, this music was described as Good Music, which at times related to some classical as well. Then the term "Easy Listening" was brought into the picture.

It was our competitor, Jim Schulke, who instituted the term "Beautiful Music." It's one which I never liked and tried to avoid using, especially on the air. It's always been my belief that beauty is in the eye or ear of the beholder. It's not for me to tell the listener that it's beautiful; let them tell me! Then I can be pleased knowing that I am making them happy and bringing joy to their lives.

While the 1960s had been a banner decade for recordings of "our kind of music," at the end of the 1970s, we faced the challenge of a lack of new recordings necessary to keep our musical sound fresh. Earlier in the 1970s, American record companies had pretty much stopped releasing recordings of artists like Percy Faith, Andre Kostelanetz, Ferrante & Teicher, and the Living Strings, and the European companies were beginning to follow suit. Thankfully, we still had a trickle from the likes of the three great French orchestral arranger-conduc-

Well-known English conductor-arranger Norrie Paramor stopped by our suite during a broadcast industry convention to thank us for including his many recordings in our repertoire.

tors, Caravelli, Franck Pourcel, and Paul Mauriat, who combined made a major contribution during this period to the body of recordings in our genre of music. Even so, most of these artists, including some outstanding English artists like Norrie Paramor, were not being distributed here in America, so we were importing them directly from the source.

About this time, we connected with another entity, an English company named Rediffusion, which was recording good arrangements of newer titles. We were able to lease a fair quantity of selections from them. It was what I would describe as the equivalent of Muzak and served the rest of the world beyond North America. They employed many different talented conductor-arrangers of the day in England to produce a quality product, a step above what is generally thought of as the quality of Muzak at the time. We availed ourselves of a fair number of their recordings, yet the master tapes we received identified only the song titles. There was no artist information provided, so this collection was simply identified under the generic name *Buckingham Strings*.

While this was a good stopgap measure, the only real route was to employ capable arranger/conductors to create arrangements to our specifications and then assemble an orchestra and go into a studio and record. Over the next several years, we worked primarily with John Fox and Nick Ingman in London and Lex De Azevedo and Pat Valentino in California, amassing a library of several hundred selections. I generally took care of the London sessions while Dave Verdery handled California, with several staffers submitting and voting on titles that we should cover.

Even though I liked and respected the work of all four of these gentlemen, John Fox became my favorite. In my opinion, no one else quite had the ability that John possessed for creating an instrumental arrangement of a pop song that conveyed and reflected the same "feeling" as the original hit vocal.

Maestro John Fox and his wife Joy during a visit to Tenafly, New Jersey.

Over the eight years that we'd work with John—which pretty much spanned the period when our Bonneville organization commissioned these exclusive recordings—I became very good friends with John and his wife Joy. As the years passed, I began staying in their home, rather than a hotel, when we were recording his sessions in London.

As an aside, Nick Ingman liked working with well-respected English recording engineer Adrian Kerridge, so his recordings were done at Landsdowne Studios, which Adrian owned. Because the studio was rather small, it couldn't hold all of the players in the large orchestra Nick used for our sessions. However, they had an interesting solution: the percussion sat in the studio's kitchen, which was located on a mezzanine level and had a large window which looked down into the studio, and these musicians wore headphones.

By the late 1970s, we'd built a fairly significant list of client stations and, at the time, didn't see much opportunity for increasing that list within the two Easy Listening/Beautiful Music formats we were offering. Having built name recognition and a reputation for delivering quality service by a talented staff, we decided to explore the possibility of supporting stations in other genres with a variety of consulting services, including market analysis and research, format structuring, computer-generated playlists and maximization of technical facilities. While we did achieve some success in this realm, we found it to be more of a distraction than the returns warranted.

In 1981, a new company, Satellite Music Network, was preparing to launch two satellite-delivered around-the-clock music formats; the first ever. We decided to join them and renamed ourselves, this time changing to Bonneville Broadcasting System—a name more in keeping with a live-programming operation. This would offer our

MRT & BBC Poster

clients the opportunity to be fed by satellite rather than reloading reels of tape every couple of hours. A number of our stations in a variety of market sizes did sign on for this service, plus new clients came aboard as well. While our headquarters were in Tenafly, a community in northern New Jersey not far from the George Washington Bridge, this operation required us to employ a group of operators to feed our programming into the satellite from the Satellite Music Network facility south of Chicago in Mokena, Illinois.

Operating a live feed like this brought about a whole new set of requirements with regard to timing. In every quarter hour, there needed to be a break to allow for a station ID plus two minutes for commercials. Hence, we had to create a large collection of two-minute musical selections which would play during these two-minute intervals, as not every station would have commercials to fill these breaks. We continued this service for about three years, until it became evident that many of the stations, especially in the larger markets, were better off having the tape library, as things simply went more smoothly when everything was under their local control.

The mid-1980s saw Bonneville acquiring our prime competitors in the format, one at a time. First was Darrel Peters' FM 100 operation, named after the Chicago station out of which it grew. Not much changed, as each division continued to service their own client stations. However eventually, the operations and production side, led by my longtime Bonneville associate Walter Powers, was merged with the Peters operation in Chicago. Next came the Schulke entity, which had been renamed Stereo Radio Productions (SRP), as it had been sold to the Cox Broadcasting folks, and one that I was much more involved in.

As soon as we began talking with the SRP stations, we learned that their biggest concern was the vast amount of complaints coming from listeners regarding repetition, i.e., the repeating of the same songs and arrangements much too frequently, which was caused by three factors: a) there were too few tapes in their library; b) there were numerous recordings that had been inserted in their library multiple times; and c) many of their tapes were playing at the same time every day. We quickly repackaged and distributed several reels with fresh music, and thanks to Walter's astute scheduling adjustments, we put this issue to rest in about a week's time.

Finally, Churchill Productions in Phoenix was acquired. Its founder, Tom Churchill, was another pioneer not only within the format but in FM broadcasting as well. It was Tom's own station, KRFM, that our client KMEO had overtaken ratings-wise more than a decade earlier.

In the late 1980s, changes were beginning to occur within the format and the industry; the management of our parent Bonneville International Corporation had changed, plus I was beginning to become bored and in need of a break. Since I was coming to the end of a contract, I elected to "retire" from the company and leave broadcasting... sort of (details in Chapter 12).

Regarding industry changes, many of our stations were seeing their management being taken over by new, younger individuals who had no real love for or understanding of the format. If they were in a market where listenership was being surveyed and reported, their reaction was to seek modifications in the programming to attract younger people to their station. It was a no-win situation from our end, as any changes that would be sufficient to bring in these new, "more desirable" listeners would irritate and drive away a fair portion of the existing audience.

Even though my direct connection to the radio business was rather limited through the 1990s, this genre continued to be my favorite. I even packaged albums of some of the great instrumental recordings we had produced at Bonneville, which were sold through gift and other specialty shops, and on a few occasions, I produced albums of Christmas melodies which a number of stations used as a promotional item to raise funds for a local charity.

At the same time, my programming philosophy remained intact at several stations across the country, and my quarter-hour programmed segments continued to be played on at least a couple of stations, including KAHM in Prescott, Arizona, a full decade after I had originally created them.

It wasn't far into the 1990s that stations began leaving the format to go a different direction in an attempt to bring younger listeners to their stations. That was the demographic the advertising community was seeking and station managements were under constant pressure to increase revenues. This, of course, had a negative impact on the division, leading Bonneville corporate to make the decision to sell; this was completed in 1993.

CHAPTER 11

It's All About the Melody

E ven though I would go on to program two other musical formats on satellite radio, my image and historical position in the industry—as is likely obvious to you by this point—is tied very much to the format that's been called Good Music, Easy Listening, and Beautiful Music. At the same time, let me note that it's also derogatorily called "elevator music" or "dentist office music" and even compared with Muzak, the background music that filled so many public spaces through the latter part of the 20th century. However, in more recent years, "elevator music" has become a descriptive term used endearingly by any number of persons who love this genre of music, as they've found no better term for describing it.

I have always vehemently objected to my version of this radio format being judged or considered comparable to what is heard in such locations or from such a source as Muzak. While it was very acceptable as a background accompaniment for a variety of activities, our programming would not naturally fade away and could easily be sung along with, as we played arrangements that stood out and had a higher average tempo than what most others offered, especially Schulke/SRP.

This format is most successful when it is a consistent around-the-clock presentation so it can function as a "utility"; it can be treated like electric light, with a switch that allows it to be easily turned on and off as the listener pleases without any further thought or decision. And, many listeners would play the station or channel from morning 'til night.

Other than the couple of tunes discussed in the WDVR section, I don't remember there being any recordings that brought questions and comments from any quantity of listeners—and we had many listeners—during my days in Philadelphia and at WJIB in Boston.

However, this changed upon my arrival in New York. Sometime in the fall of 1969, while rummaging through WRFM's extensive record library, I came across Greek folk singer Nana Mouskouri's recording of the Mexican mariachi tune "Cu-cu-ru-cu-cu Paloma." I was aware of the song and knew that it had been recorded by Perry Como and other vocalists, but I had never paid much attention to it. I put Nana's disc on the turntable and listened and found it intriguing.

Nana, during a visit to New York City in the mid-1960's (Courtesy Nana's personal collection)

Into the studio we headed, asking the host on duty to play it in place of the next scheduled vocal. He set it up and began to listen on the cue system, immediately turning up his nose and declaring that if we play recordings like this, the station would lose listeners rather than gaining new ones. I said, "Let's play it and see how it fits." Before it had finished, listeners were calling, asking who the singer was, what the name of the album was and where to buy it. It became a staple of our format and continued to be for me as well, right into the Sirius XM days. None of the WRFM air staff ever questioned one of my musical choices again.

I'm not sure whether you'd call the content of my version of this format an eclectic mix of melodies, arrangements, and instrumentation, but I was always on the prowl for something different, usually a sound or a recording featuring an unusual instrument, such as the panpipes. It's all a part of what you'd call a process of music discovery.

Even when I was managing enLighten, Sirius XM's Southern Gospel music channel, I was sensitive to artists and songs which were not destined for or had not made the hit charts; in this format, it was as much about the message of the song as it was the melody. In a fair number of cases, recordings that fell into this category became favorites, because of their unique message or because the message touched a listener's heart with regard to a situation being faced at the moment.

As an aside, after enLighten became available on satellite, there was much rejoicing in the Southern Gospel community. However, it wasn't long before we began receiving complaints, all carrying the same message: "Why are you playing all these groups we never heard of?" Now, mind you, the groups and soloists we played—other than the few cited above—were the major names within the genre, both current and historically. However, it wasn't much more than thirty days before our emails mostly read, "Wow, what an education we're getting—we've never heard most of these wonderful artists before!" This occurred because the listeners did not have a local station playing any Southern Gospel, so their primary exposure to this music was groups that came to their area for concerts.

Jerry Del Colliano, the early employee at WDVR who went on to great success in radio and the media, recently commented: "Music discovery is the one thing the music-loving audience really wants from radio." From the earliest days, it's been one of my guiding principles: looking for interesting melodies or differing sounds or instruments that would capture my listeners' fancy—as was the case with Nana Mouskouri and the songs/recordings discussed below. They are what we who worked with the format called "turntable favorites" or "tape recorder hits," described that way because they were melodies that had become special with our audience yet had never been pop chart hits as such.

At the same time, I was always looking for ways to stretch the boundaries of the musical format, not in an effort to bring in younger listeners but rather to increase the variety of what we played in order to enhance the pleasure of the listener.

In 1994, writer and musical enthusiast Joseph Lanza published a book titled *Elevator Music*, in which I am quoted as saying:

I played a song called "Dolannes Melody" by Jean-Claude Borelly that had a panpipe. People started calling in asking what the instrument was. Nobody ever heard it before. I later picked out "The Lonely Shepherd" performed by Zamfir with the James Last Orchestra. It was an unfamiliar melody which drove the listeners crazy. We generated as many as 15 to 20 calls a day for a single play. Nobody else was playing it. My peers told me it was nuts, but the listeners loved it. After that, Zamfir sold over 500,000 albums in television promotions alone.

While "Dolannes Melody" and Jean-Claude Borelly were popular among the tens of thousands of listeners we had across the nation during the 1970s and 1980s, it was more the melody than the panpipes which attracted attention—partly because Jean-Claude recorded two versions of the song, the second one featuring a trumpet, and we played them almost interchangeably.

The panpipes, also known as a pan flute, is an ancient eastern European instrument said to have had its origins several thousand years ago. The album containing "The Lonely Shepherd" arrived in my hands in 1976 or 1977. The moment I heard Zamfir's playing, along with the James Last Orchestra and James Last's arrangement, there was no question in my mind; it went into play as quickly as possible.

Gheorghe Zamfir and his panpipes

One of the things we expected our client stations to do was to keep a log of calls from listeners about the music, noting the song title, the artist, and time of day the call came in. It was about this time that Bonneville International acquired KRON-FM from the *Chronicle* newspaper folks in San Francisco and renamed it KOIT (naming it after the Coit Tower, a San Francisco landmark), at which time it began offering our programming. Even though it was fairly new and competing against the well-entrenched KABL-AM and FM, one week when we received their listener call log, I could hardly believe what I saw: after Zamfir's "Lonely Shepherd" had played one morning at around 3:00 a.m., the announcer on duty logged fourteen calls about the song, the instrument, and the artist. Our stations received so many calls inquiring about the instrument that we finally sent out a fact sheet about the panpipe and its origins, since it wasn't familiar to most folks here in North America.

Two recordings that crossed our path in the 1970s which became listener favorites, are ones that were first discovered by Phil Stout (who passed away as I was writing this in early 2016), my former associate at WDVR in Philadelphia. He went on—as mentioned— to become the music programmer for our arch-competitor Schulke Radio Productions. The recordings were Caravelli's recording of "Wigwam," which was written by folk-rock artist Bob Dylan; and "Music From Across the Way," which was originally known as "The Last Guest Is Gone," by James Last. Two or three other orchestras recorded arrangements of "Wigwam," which we played; however, none of them caught the listeners' fancy. There was just something about the Caravelli arrangement.

After "The Last Guest Is Gone" became a favorite of Easy Listening radio listeners, James Last, the German conductor/composer whose real first name is Hansi and who spent much of his later years living in Florida, wrote words for the melody as "Music From Across the Way" and recorded a vocal version with his choral group. On a personal note, the instrumental recording of this melody is what brought my beloved Alicia and me back together after an absence of sixteen years. She heard it played regularly on the SRP station in Philadelphia and just had to have the record. She called the station and several record shops without success, so finally turned to the man she knew could deliver! (We had little contact over those sixteen years, but each always seemed to know how to reach the other one.) I did deliver the recording a couple of weeks later—in person— and that was pretty much it. We soon picked up where we had broken off in 1958 after I was drafted into the military. (For the record, during these intervening years, I had a marriage that lasted a little over a decade and produced three children, none of whom has chosen broadcasting as a career.)

In a similar case... the other extremely popular German bandleader, Bert Kaempfert, composed a tune he titled "Moon Over Naples" in 1965. Within the next year, another songwriter would take the melody and add lyrics, changing its title to "Spanish Eyes." It was soon recorded by several vocalists and would become one of the most popular songs of the late 20th century.

From the early 1970s right on up through the years, English vocalist Roger Whittaker was a favorite of many listeners. They flocked to his concerts, traveling many miles in some cases, whenever he came to America. I can't think of a particular song that stood out above others, but we regularly played "The Last Farewell," "I Don't Believe In 'If' Anymore," "Durham Town," and "You Are My Miracle," most written by Roger himself.

Speaking of Roger, early in the 1980s he was the artist to introduce "Wind Beneath My Wings" to the world. It immediately became a favorite of thousands of music lovers and was soon recorded by numerous vocalists, but it did not reach hit status until it was released by Bette Midler nearly five years later. We did not initially play the recording by Roger; instead, we chose an arrangement that had been recorded by singer Vic Damone for the aforementioned Darrel Peters to play in his programming service which, as noted, was later acquired by Bonneville International. It became one more vocal which received a great positive reaction from listeners.

It took a long time and much listening before I found another song by Nana Mouskouri that I felt our audience would "turn on" to. Nana spoke, sang, and recorded albums in any number of different languages. However, I never felt very good about her English-language recordings; it was my feeling that whoever was responsible for producing these recordings was failing her. Finally, in the 1980s she released a new album containing a song titled "Even Now." It was finally the one that was worthy of being an encore to "Cu-cu-ru-cu-cu Paloma." And, it was as big a hit, if not bigger, with the listeners. At virtually the same time, pop singer Barry Manilow released a new single titled none other than "Even Now." However, they are totally different songs.

Earlier, I mentioned going to London for recording sessions with John Fox, which we did about twice a year. Most every conductor has a favorite place to work, and his was CTS, a large recording facility that sat next to the famed Wembley Stadium in north London. John's sessions, which involved around thirty-five musicians, were always done in CTS's largest studio, which could handle upwards of a hundred musicians and was used for recording the orchestral scores of numerous motion pictures over the years.

One day, as I was walking down a hallway there, a gentleman stopped me and asked if I was the American radio person working with John Fox. When I answered in the affirmative, he introduced himself as Dick Bakker from Holland and handed me his album entitled, "Around the World." The one selection from this album that became a favorite is "Mull of Kintyre." We've played other recordings of this Paul McCartney melody—which John Fox told me is based on a couple of different Scottish folk tunes—but Dick's, with a chorus featuring a bagpipe sound, is most people's choice to hear.

Dick has done numerous other recordings, including several under the name of the Botticelli Orchestra, providing a great collection of material perfect for our genre and still well-loved and played today.

Another for this list of "tape recorder hits" is "Ballad for Adeline" as played by German pianist Richard Clayderman. When he first came on the scene, I looked upon him as a young Liberace, as several of his album covers included a candelabra.

Finally, I must note another vocal, this one by Abba, the Swedish quartet. We've played several of their songs over the years, including their hit "Fernando." However, the one that most captured our listeners' interest is "I Have A Dream." I don't remember it as being a hit in the pop world, but it certainly was for us. Listeners would normally call their local station with their music questions. If those station folks could not come up with an answer, they'd often give out the 800 number for our

Tenafly, New Jersey, headquarters. For this song, for some reason, listeners did not pick up on the title line; rather, they'd catch a line that repeated in the song several times, which is "I believe in angels." This stumped the local air staff, so our receptionist Marge received numerous calls most every time it played on the stations. It became so frequent that, almost before the caller could utter "I believe in angels," Marge would give them the song title, the artist, and the record album name and number.

One major orchestral favorite is Caravelli's arrangement of the "Midnight Blue Theme," based on Ludwig von Beethoven's Piano Sonata no. 8, known as the *Pathetique* sonata. It is one of the most-asked-about melodies that we played on Sirius XM's Escape, as it was when we first played it on stations across America in the 1980s. The vocal version of this song became a major hit in France in the 1980s, which I'm sure is what led Maestro Caravelli to record his own arrangement of the melody.

Even though satellite receivers display the names of the artist and the song being played, I heard from many who were seeking to purchase a copy but had not been able to find it. As is the case with Caravelli's "Wigwam," both of these were released prior to the origin of the compact disc. While a fair number of Caravelli selections have been reissued on CD, neither of these two has, frustrating many, as they are at or near the top of the list of favorites among all the songs that the maestro ever recorded, at least with American music lovers.

Yours truly in one of his favorite places, the music library.

Another orchestral favorite is "Chi Mai," which was composed and recorded by Ennio Morriconi. While it was used in a couple of films and another TV production, it gained recognition and popularity when featured in the BBC 1981 documentary, *The Life and Times of David Lloyd George,* who was Great Britain's Prime Minister during the World War I period.

These are just a few of the unique recordings that we played over the years which drew the greatest response from our listeners; yet, there certainly are at least another couple of dozen which made the list of "tape recorder hits." In this traditional format realm, too many think that it's a no-brainer—play anything that is within the genre and fits some artificial parameters and you've got it made. In reality, my sense was that a great melody was the foundation, and it needed to be delivered through a great arrangement which communicated the message the composer embodied in that melody he or she was led to write.

Another factor which I believe contributed to our success was a willingness to stretch the boundaries where my instinct said it was appropriate. This was always done on a song-by-song or particular recording basis, never a universal action simply because a recording was by a particular artist. One such case arose in the mid-1980s; I pondered whether I'd be going beyond the logical boundaries to air this song, as it was a solo vocal and was, by far, the most aggressive vocal arrangement we'd ever played. Yet something about it grabbed me personally, so I felt many listeners

Tony Bennett, paying a visit to our new Bonneville Broadcast Consultants facility in Tenafly, New Jersey, in 1974. (Courtesy Greg Katkowski collection)

would feel the same way. From the 1980s version of the movie, "The Jazz Singer," it was Neil Diamond singing "America." Can't you just hear it: "... they're coming to America!" At the time, we had well over 100 stations across the nation playing the format with millions of listeners tuned in, and I cannot recall receiving a single complaint.

I don't know how others feel but, to me, there's a patriotic aspect to this song. From my youth, the patriotic tunes of America—such as "God Bless the U. S. A." and "I'm A Yankee Doodle Dandy"—can be counted among my favorites. Hearing one immediately evokes an emotional response.

In my lifetime, I haven't met many so-called "celebrities," nor can I say that I've had a great desire to, unless they've had a particular connection to my programming. However, I've had many celebrities of a different kind in my life; they are the songs I've been able to uncover and play for those who have listened to my programming over these past fifty-plus years. Discovering gems to which the listeners would react in the manner I've described here warmed my heart over and over.

One of the most popular artists in the Easy Listening genre (one I mentioned earlier), an artist that we first began to play on WDVR in the early 1960s and that is still heard frequently on Sirius XM's Escape channel, is Bert Kaempfert. While not a composer, I consider myself a professional listener, possessing a listening sensitivity likely anointed by God... as it is my ability to listen to the work of those like Bert with the ears of the masses, choosing selections I believe will be enjoyed by those who listen. That being said, I recently read this quote from Bert, with which I feel total empathy: "I want to make music for everyone.

It's meant to give people pleasure. If it doesn't, it's failed in its purpose." This reminds me of the wonderfully appropriate slogan for Tower Records, the record retailer that was once big in the U.S. as well as in overseas places like Brazil and Japan: "No Music... No Life!"

Let me echo that sentiment with a loud amen!

CHAPTER 12
The "In-Between" Years

hortly before my planned retirement from Bonneville at the end of 1987, an independent radio show producer had conceived a weekly program designed for Easy Listening stations titled Special of the Week, and I was invited to sign on as its music director. This was a new challenge that would keep my creative juices fired up, as each show would require three or four tunes for each of the eight themed segments.

Each week, we'd come up with the topics to be spotlighted on the show. While we had no trouble finding interesting subjects, there were times when it was a challenge to find musical titles that supported the chosen theme. After I completed this process, Ken

Lamb, who was one of our announcer/hosts at WRFM, would create and record the narration for the two-hour program.

In its early years, the show was well received by both station management and listeners alike. I served in this role for about two years. However, with the arrival of the 1990s, it began losing stations, as more and more the Easy Listening format was being dropped in favor of programming with younger demographic appeal.

Most of these stations were not losing listeners or seeing their ratings decrease. The issue was that the advertising community decided that people over fifty were not good candidates for their clients' products, partly because "older people" spend less money and partly because they become set in their ways as to which brands they buy and are not open to change.

At the same time, I let my emotional desire to own a radio station take control of my actions, overruling common sense and good judgment. In plain words, I took step after step, made decision after decision that, as the broadcast consultant I had been previously for nearly twenty years, I would have advised anyone else *not to do*!

This led me to acquire a full-time AM station, KRSS, in Spokane, Washington, a market I did not know and did not investigate carefully before jumping in. Upon visiting, however, I found it a very likeable community. The price was right and the format it was airing, contemporary Christian music, fired my enthusiasm. I had a sincere interest in the genre even though it was not one I was really knowledgeable about. The seller convinced me that it was on the right track and that all that was needed was additional funding to make some technical improvements and to support an increased sales and promotional effort. I bit!

My first mistakes were failing to move to the market and waiting too long to install a manager who was committed to the mission, which included bringing the station to a self-support-ing position. Considering that there were two other AM stations which were off the air at the time due to financial problems, this was to be a nearly insurmountable challenge. So, after two years, we did the only smart thing: returned the license to the former owner and "got out of town."

I cannot remember how I connected with him, but I must recognize a gentleman named Mark Pluimer who, with no guar-antees from me, came over from a station in South Dakota which had a similar format and operational situation and which was doing very well. Mark used virtually every approach conceivable to—in honest terms—save the station, as much for the listeners, who had no other options, as for my sake.

I still occasionally wonder whether, if we had moved to the market, taken on day-to-day management, and totally in-volved ourselves in the Christian community and events where potential listeners and supporters were present, we could have brought about a different outcome. Considering that KRSS was an AM station with a non-mass appeal format competing against several TV stations along with more than a dozen radio stations, both FM and AM, I still come to the conclusion that it would have been a tough long-term challenge that was more than likely to end negatively. This was especially the case when you factor in that Spokane did not have a particularly strong economy at the time.

Before I move on from this Spokane story, I've got to share

a little of the interesting technical aspects of this facility, located at 1230 on the dial and alleged as being Spokane's first radio station dating to 1921. It's had multiple call letters and programming formats over its lifetime but (and I'm not sure what its setup was previously) from the 1950s through today, its transmitting tower and facility have been on the roof of a building in downtown Spokane. AM stations normally have their towers in an open area outside the center of their community, although this rooftop approach was apparently fairly common back in the earlier days of AM radio. Today, few are left—although I've confirmed that other such facilities are still operating

The transmitting antenna, sitting atop the multi-story Delaney Building (Courtesy Philco Bill)

in Baltimore, Maryland, Scranton, Pennsylvania, Lowell, Massachusetts, and High Point, North Carolina, plus more than one in the Chicago, Illinois, area.

Getting a little more technical for a moment, AM station transmitting antenna systems have two components: not only do they have one or more of the very visible towers, they have one hundred or more "radial" wires that fan out from the base of each tower like spokes on a bicycle wheel for a distance equal to the height of the tower. Without both pieces, the station's signal is severely hampered. In recent years, tower sites in remote locations lacking good security have been targets of thieves who have profited from stealing and selling this valuable copper wire.

In the case of these rooftop operations, they still must have these horizontal wires stretching in all directions, normally requiring them to be attached to adjoining buildings. In our Spokane situation, many of the neighboring buildings to which they were previously attached had been torn down, causing the station to lose about seventy-five percent of these lines. However, it didn't appear to have any impact on the station's coverage day or night.

After I'd extracted us from the Spokane fiasco and after my association with the Special of the Week production had ended, I devoted myself to activities which Alicia and I had planned for some time. She is an accomplished vocalist, and it was her desire to have my support in the concert schedule she'd begun shortly after our moving from northern New Jersey to Bucks County, Pennsylvania, in 1987. Still, my heart would not completely let go of my passion for radio.

Earlier, I mentioned WNEW-AM. It was a station that was legendary in New York City, with a tremendous history as a pacesetter and a ground-breaker in music and personality radio, and it was one of the format's pioneers dating back to 1935. Unfortunately, the glory days had ended several decades earlier. The station had deviated more and more from its heritage, which WRFM had capitalized on and benefited from in 1969 and 1970, as we were building the station into a powerhouse audience-wise.

At the end of the 1970s, smart new management came on board and sought to take the station back to its programming roots, yet they did not bring in a programmer who truly understood what the musical content needed to be in order to have a shot at being successful. While it still had a group of credible personalities, the overall format was being executed quite poorly and its musical playlist was drastically out of sync with what it was supposedly attempting to achieve, as its poor ratings confirmed.

It was my belief that WNEW, even though it was an AM in a world that had increasingly turned to FM, still had solid potential for attracting a much greater listenership than it had at that time. I approached the general manager and, based on my long record of success, especially in the mature audience realm, was hired as the station's programming and music consultant.

I quickly set out to prepare a strategy and build a list of recordings to be played. However, I never got the opportunity to prove what my concepts could achieve, as the general manager was not committed to fulfilling the rest of his obligation: convincing the air staff and requiring them to cooperate. They simply wanted to continue doing it their way and playing the music they and their friends liked, and the general manager chose not to do battle. Hence, I saw no positive benefits to continuing my involvement.

When you are playing the wrong music and are a music-oriented station, it doesn't really matter how well or poorly you do the rest. In a market of more than ten million people, only a small percentage of them live and play in the Greenwich Village section of Manhattan. This is where I found the station to have its greatest problem: playing to this small community rather than to the vast audience that lay beyond!

In my opinion, the broader market would be attracted to a musical playlist populated by mainstream non-rock artists rang-ing from Doris Day to the Carpenters, Nat King Cole to Bobby Darin, Rosemary Clooney to Barbra Streisand and Perry Como to Neil Diamond. Instead, the playlist was featuring more obscure artists from the jazz, lounge, and cabaret idioms.

While I was committed to making WNEW a station of note once again in the New York region and had confidence we could accomplish it, I did not have the motivation to attempt to sell my concepts to (or, in plain words, do battle with) the air staff.

It was not long afterward that the general manager departed, and within a year or so, as the station was not producing a positive cash flow, the uncooperative musical hosts would be unemployed as their once-great facility was sold to billionaire Michael Bloomberg, who turned it into WBBR, which airs a financial news format.

So, over the next few years, I was not actively involved in the radio industry. Still, as time passed into the latter half of the 1990s, I found myself missing that involvement and began searching for an opportunity to again make a difference in radio, which was once more going through massive changes. Dozens of stations in larger markets were being gobbled up by group owners thanks to an increase in station ownership limits passed by the Federal Communications Commission. But in 1996, my interest had turned toward connecting with a station in my regional area that was suffering from a lack of listeners and lack of advertising–of which there were several–and instituting a number of promotional and programming concepts that had been germinating in my head for quite some time.

As I had in the earlier days of my career, I began by choosing a particular station with the thought that they could really use my services and wondering whether they would allow me to help.

My first focus was a new AM station under construction just across the river from where I was living. It had a good middle-of-the-dial position with a solid full-time signal that would cover two counties with the highest median household incomes in the nation, neither of which had a broadcast station providing local service—very different from the situation we had faced in Spokane. Here's what I had conceived as a plan for building a successful small-market station:

- To begin attracting attention, as soon as the technical facility was completed, put an endless tape loop on the air, listing every single community and village located within the projected service area.
- Do what political campaigns call "boots on the ground": visit every retail business within this area and tell them about the station and its plans. (The long-term goal is to get every business on the air as an advertiser, no matter how small a schedule.)
- Other than a morning host who was a good interviewer, have the primary air staff be news reporters providing local information at least twice an hour, with the bulk of weekday air time filled with syndicated talk shows.
- Because this is an area with lots of art galleries and antique shops, create relevant weekend programming that would be of interest to the many tourists coming out from "the city."

- Promote the station to the visitors on their way in. The majority of these visitors would be traveling down one main highway, and it so happened that along this road was a crane rental business. Since most of the cranes were on the property on weekends and sitting right by the highway, why not make a deal to have a couple of these cranes hold up a large billboard advertising the station and its frequency?

This all proved to be a hypothetical concept, as the two young gentlemen who were constructing the station with "Daddy's money" had their own ideas. They were hiring a crew of DJs who would play an adult contemporary musical format. Gaining little in the way of listenership and advertising, they soon leased the station to a regional group operator, who made a minor improvement: they installed three talk show hosts who filled thirteen hours each weekday. This was a good start in the programming area; however, these gentlemen spent ninety-five percent of their air time talking to themselves, as there were few callers. Why? There was no visible advertising or promotional activities to bring attention to the station and connect with the community's residents.

During this time, I was able to meet with a senior executive of the group operator. The meeting did not prove productive, as the gentleman appeared to have little comprehension of the principles of successful radio station operation and could not understand how I could help them.

After several months, in the middle of one day, the local talk programming was gone and the station became a satellite of another of the group's stations. In the twenty years since that day, the station has had multiple owners and a multitude of format changes, none of which has delivered meaningful local service to this affluent area.

What none of these people seemed to recognize is how vital it is to constantly be on the lookout for innovative ways to promote your station; to command people's attention. At no time in my career did I have sufficient funds to spend on major advertising or promotional campaigns. So, when dollars aren't in ready supply, it's time for ingenuity.

Let me qualify my proposed plan: I believed it was totally on focus for that time and that situation. I'm not prepared to say whether I believe these concepts or promotional methods, if tried today, would work. However, the philosophy behind them and a continual proactive approach, along with being constantly vigilant about creating an on-going "wow" factor, will play a giant role in your personal and business success. If you don't believe me, ask Jerry Lee in Philadelphia. For more than fifty years, Jerry has led the privately owned FM station—which began as WDVR, later became WEAZ and now WBEB—as a ratings and revenue leader against competition from several powerful group owners in this, one of the nation's top metropolitan areas. (Sadly, as noted earlier, station founder David L. Kurtz passed away in November of 2005, after which Jerry acquired full ownership.)

Yes, there are situations where, as at WRFM, word-of-mouth can be very helpful. But it doesn't happen on its own; there's got to be some kind of publicity to cause folks to tune in and then be motivated enough to tell others.

Not long after we returned to Pennsylvania, a station very

close to where we were living was being sold. Shortly after the announcement, I met with the purchaser to discuss consulting for or managing the station. However, it wasn't long afterward that it was announced that he had signed on with a consultant who was proposing a format of music made up of "recordings that were selected based on sounding good on AM radio!" Somehow, that concept didn't add up or compute for me, as the time for a local AM station to be successful airing a pure music format was rapidly passing in the late 1980s, considering that the area was served by more than two dozen music-formatted FM stations.

The station had been airing programming that made total sense for this unique, upscale suburban community, a format made up of some music but heavy on local news and information and local sports. What it needed was not a new format but an upgrading of its content and staff quality-wise, plus better promotion to bolster its image. What it and its community got was another badly programmed radio station which ended up with no listeners and no advertising revenue.

It finally went silent for an extended period while its antenna system was rebuilt. Upon returning, it instituted a network-delivered twenty-four-hour-a-day all-news format with virtually zero local content being inserted.

All through this period, I'd sent the owner an occasional letter and left him telephone messages, offering him help. He never once responded. Finally, after ten years of ownership, he decided to sell through an auction to be held in the station's parking lot. Alicia and I attended along with a local businessman who was interested in acquiring it... at the right price.

Once the bidding passed that level, he was out, and it eventually was sold for double that amount, which I still believe was much more than the property was worth. Afterward, I spoke to the seller, who recognized me. The only thing he could say was, "Marlin, where were you when we needed you?" I was dumbfounded, so much so that I had no reply. He was always known as an astute businessman, so I wonder if his secretary "protected" him by disposing of mail and messages she felt he didn't need to see.

I continued to pray, "God, please grant me the opportunity to have one more grand gig in this industry that I love before I am too old and feeble physically and mentally to handle the challenge." One day, a large ad appeared seeking a vice president of radio for a public TV-radio operation in a medium-sized market. Included was a full page of qualifications, which I fully met except for one. I'd never worked for a National Public Radio station. As they continually flew in candidates from NPR stations across the country, the president of the organization would not interview me. He finally acknowledged that his concern was that "his staff would not respect me," supposedly because I was not from the public radio sphere. They eventually hired a salesperson from a local commercial station who had grown up in the market and was very involved in community activities and organizations: absolutely the most logical person to choose for the position!

In spite of investing a great deal of time and energy in presenting myself as qualified for the stations' needs in a number of situations, even though I had a fairly solid reputation as a successful broadcaster, my efforts had not borne much fruit.

(I've always said that finding a job is a full-time job.) However, the skies were beginning to brighten, even though the pursuit would require nearly two years of patience!

CHAPTER 13
Satellite Radio

I t was in 1998 that I first read in a trade publication about something called SDARS—satellite radio—for which the U.S. government had just issued two licenses. In the story, it was mentioned that one of the licensees, which would soon be named XM Satellite Radio, had brought in well-known radio programming guru Lee Abrams to head up its programming and creative operations. We didn't really know each other personally—we come from the opposite ends of the musical and radio programming spectrum—and had only met once very briefly; however, we knew each other by reputation, as we had both had our accomplishments written about in trade publications.

While it was a new startup venture, I felt that if Lee saw it as an opportunity, it was worth my investigating. Actually, I hadn't had much success convincing owners of traditional radio stations that I could help them. I contacted Lee, and he invited me to stop by if I was coming to Washington, D.C., where the company was based, which I did Thanksgiving week of 1998. Lee told me some of their plans and that the XM Radio name had just been finalized that morning ("There was AM, then FM, now XM," he said.). However, a location for the broadcast facility had not yet been determined, so hiring of programmers was at least a year or more away, but Lee suggested that I keep in touch. I did this by sending him notes from time to time, always including something I thought he'd find of interest.

In 2000, reading that a building had been secured and construction begun, I called him and he asked me to call his assistant, Dave Logan, in April. This I did and was told that there were no plans for including the Easy Listening/Beautiful Music format in the initial lineup of 100 channels; however, he once again asked me to "stay in touch." I did this about once a month until around August and, after reading of numerous programming hires, concluded I was being strung along, so I stopped calling.

Then, in mid-November, exactly two years after my first contact with Lee, I came home to find a voice mail message from a lady named Lori Parkerson, who identified herself as Dave Logan's secretary. The message said that Dave Logan wanted to see me and asked how soon I could get on the Metroliner and get to Washington (we were living in Bucks County, Pennsylvania, at the time). Wow... what had changed?

Two days later, I arrived at 1500 Eckington Place, N.E., at the appointed time. After waiting about a half hour, Dave Logan came dashing into the waiting area, introducing himself and handing me a hard hat, saying I'd need it to tour the broadcast area, which was still under construction, and that four others would be joining us. The tour lasted a good hour and a quarter and Dave didn't miss a detail in his sales pitch.

At the tour's conclusion, he dispatched the others and took me back to his office. Upon closing the door, he asked, "Do you have any questions?" My reply was that he'd told me there were no plans for an Easy Listening channel, so

I would first visit this building in November 2000 and it would become my base of operations for just shy of the next fifteen years.

what did they have in mind for me? "You're an expert on the 40s; we'd like you to program our 1940s/Big Band channel" was his answer. While I was not truly an expert on that era of music, I certainly was aware of many of the artists and knew the hit songs from that period. It didn't take much thought for me to realize this was an opportunity and a great challenge that I could handle, even though there was the matter of our moving to the nation's capital. Would Alicia be amenable to such a move? Even though I'd managed a successful New York City radio station and was the founder and president of an organization that programmed hundreds of stations, I felt quite appreciative that Lee and Dave were inviting me to join their team of top professional radio programmers. Although I was old enough by then to collect Social Security, I would again have the opportunity to do what I have always loved best: create programming that would be meaningful and bring joy to the lives of those who became our listeners.

Because it would give her husband the opportunity to

return to the field of endeavor which was his passion, Alicia agreed to the move. So, two weeks after being offered this position, I joined the XM team on Monday morning, December 4th. On this day, all these years later, I'd be harkening back to the early days of my career and joining another start-up operation... which would be very different from the earlier ones, as it'd be my first working in the 21st-century all-digital world of broadcasting.

Here we were, three dozen or so program directors, producers, and air personalities already in place and the numbers growing daily, so that by the spring of 2001 there'd be well over 100 individuals of all ages. I was the oldest, Dermot Hussey of the reggae channel was just two years younger, and on the other end of the spectrum, a couple of them were barely out of their teens.

This group of well-experienced individuals, each skilled in a particular genre of music or non-music type of radio programming, had been brought together for one purpose: to design and assemble top-quality content to fill 100 individual channels for 168 hours each week.

The broadcast facilities consisted of eighty-two studios of varying sizes along with the master control center, which monitors and switches studios and channels, plus row upon row of racks which held the computers and electronic components that make it all function and deliver the combined signal to two giant satellite transmission dishes. They in turn send the signal to the two satellites which sit some 22,000 miles above the equator. All of this was housed on the second floor of this hundred-year-old concrete and brick building, the former location of a printing company that, among other things, for years printed the *National Geographic* magazine.

Since it would be several months before the technical facilities would be ready for operation, we'd not have access to any of the musical recordings that had been loaded into a "giant digital tub," as I call it, nor could we begin producing any channel imaging material. Therefore, our early weeks were devoted to conceiving and planning on paper. Plus, we received multiple days of training in various computer programs, as much of what we'd do would require these skills for properly doing our jobs.

As the team continued to fill out, Lee Abrams, whose title was Chief Creative Officer, began holding full-day sessions that were called "boot camps," where discussions included branding of individual channels and terms like "ear candy." He spoke of "discovery" and bringing the listener the unexpected and being authentic. And something Lee said hit home for me, who never considered that I had a good on-air voice: "it's not how great your voice is, it's what you have to say."

What is "ear candy?" It's short bits of sound which are relevant to the genre or era in which you are programming, taking the listener on a mental experience beyond the music. It might be a line from a famous movie or a spoken line by the artist you are playing. In our case for the 1940s channel, I immediately went searching for recordings of the late-evening big band broadcasts featured on the radio networks during "our era" to extract the introductions, which gave the name of the ballroom or hotel, its location, and the name of the band.

Because England played such a big part in the European war, the Westminster chimes of Big Ben, the world-famous clock that sits atop Parliament, became one of our signature sounds after the British Embassy in Washington, D.C., kindly sent us a high-quality recording of it striking.

If you are old enough to remember life before the interstate highways, you might remember that back then, along many highways you'd come across a series of five signs containing such rhymes as:

"Approached a crossing
Without looking ...
Who will eat
His widow's cooking?
Burma-Shave"

"A man, a miss ...
A car -- a curve ...
He kissed the miss ...
And missed the curve
Burma-Shave"

We recorded a whole series of these, read by a "country highway" female voice, along with a collection of advertising commercials which were heard on radio in the 1940s; our channel was prepared to live in its era.

Recently, I read a biography of the well-known radio and TV personality from the mid-20th century, Arthur Godfrey, in which he stated his belief that we as broadcasters should educate as well as entertain. That's exactly what I was committed to doing! In that I would be creating programming devoted to one of the most important periods in the history of our nation and the world, I had to deliver a product that was more than just a jukebox.

I've always felt that branding is important, so I immediately focused on that. First, I had to recognize that the era I was dealing with was not limited to the decade of the 1940s–the channel initially having been labeled "1940's/Big Band." Considering that the heyday of the big bands began in the mid-1930s, I did not see that the standard phrase being applied to the XM Radio Decade channels truly conveyed our message. The message I came up with was rather long, but it clearly stated what we were offering: The Forties and More... On Track Number Four! Even if you never listened to the channel, you can envision where this is going. Since I grew up loving trains, and since the railroads played such a vital role during World War II and before, in hauling both freight and passengers, wouldn't it make sense to carry through with this theme in branding? Audio-wise, this would be carried out with a collection of steam locomotive whistles, which would be heard between musical selections once or twice an hour.

Following through, the brand name for the channel became the Savoy Express. "Express," of course, related to the high-speed passenger trains which were found on most railroads of the era. I had grown up next to the Reading Railroad north of Philadelphia, and

Savoy Express

watched its premier silver-colored express, the *Crusader,* pass by headed north to Jersey City, New Jersey. So it was natural to adopt its sleek visual appearance for inclusion when I commissioned a graphic artist friend, D. Jane Albanese, to create a design for imprinting on channel T-shirts.

Why the name Savoy? First, there's the song made famous in the 1930s by Benny Goodman, "Stompin' At the Savoy," which refers to the Savoy Ballroom in the Harlem section of New York City, which was one of the top dance halls in America from the 1920s into the 1950s. What made this hall so special, and the reason I chose its name for our channel, was that it was the only place in America prior to the end of World War II where dancers of all colors could dance on the same floor at the same time! However, there was one strict requirement, and if you didn't meet it, you'd quickly be tossed out: you had to be a top-notch dancer. After all, this is where the Lindy Hop (named after famed aviator Charles Lindberg, later called the jitterbug) was created, and everyone wanted to be on that floor, so there had to be rules.

As for the music, it was time to generate a list of the most popular recordings from not just a decade but the fifteen-year period beginning in 1935, when Benny Goodman's band, playing at the Palomar Ballroom in Los Angeles, let loose and set the dancers on fire, kicking off the swing era!

Meanwhile, as we entered 2001, the engineers continued wiring the broadcast facilities, and preparations were finalized for launching our first of two satellites into orbit. As we all stood by with fingers crossed, watching the live feed from the launch area—which was a floating platform situated in the Pacific Ocean south of Hawaii near the equator—the countdown progressed until with just ten seconds left before liftoff, someone on the scene shouted, "Stop!" The launch was aborted —apparently due to a malfunction in a monitoring system, not a problem with the control system itself—much to everyone's disappointment. After a launch is scrubbed, it takes nearly two months to ready the rocket for another try. Fortunately, satellite number one, known as Rock, went up without a hitch in early April, and satellite number two, known as Roll, was placed in orbit in early June. (From these names, it should be obvious where management's primary focus was.)

By early spring, we began to gain access to and receive training in the two computerized systems that were needed for managing our channels; one for scheduling the music and various elements that made up the channel's on-air structure, and the other in which the individual audio elements would be loaded and managed and which would then play them back for broadcast when called upon. We also began working with our producer in creating the non-music elements—called "imaging"—which would be key to making the Savoy Express on XM Track Number Four an aural portrait of the era it represented, rather than simply be a jukebox.

We were now on the fast track to complete the design of our channel, as the desire was for all the channels to be up and running by mid-June, even though we'd not have paying customers until sometime in September. First, we had to dig into our vast musical library—the company early on had employed an outside group to acquire and load into our system every musical CD that was commercially available at the time—and find the recordings needed for our channel. While this source did not prove to contain nearly every recording we wanted to be playing, it did provide enough to get us rolling. And we had assembled a nice group of "ear candy" pieces and station identifiers, all of which gave us the components necessary for bringing the Savoy Express to life and get it rolling down XM Track Number Four.

Meanwhile, at the XM technical center in southern Florida, a group of top-drawer digital engineers were working feverishly to finalize the receiver chip-set (the "brain" of most any kind of digital/computer device made) so that the unit could choose any of the three potential signals it could pick up: either of the two satellites or a terrestrial repeater transmitter—whichever provided the strongest signal. There are several hundred of these repeaters, situated in metropolitan areas where there are tall buildings that could block the receiving antenna from "seeing" either of the satellites.

By late August, everything had come together. Pioneer and Sony were manufacturing receivers, all 100 of XM's initial channels were operating full tilt, television commercials were produced and ready for airing in the southwestern U.S. markets where the service was to first be offered, and the launch date was set for... September 12, 2001. Naturally, on September 11 everything changed; all plans were cancelled. However, later in September, we began to make the service available.

About this time, another concept began to germinate in my mind: If this channel is celebrating and living in the era through the events and sounds of this historic time, shouldn't we be airing a daily newscast? Yes! Not just the highlights of happenings on this date throughout history—instead, present a newscast containing reports of events occurring on the current month and day in a year between 1936 and 1949. As we liked to say in this regard, "we knew General Dwight D. Eisenhower as a great World War II military leader who led the Allies to victory in Europe... we never knew he became a president of the United States!"

A fellow program director, Bill Schmalfeldt, who at the time was in charge of the Broadway channel, said that if I provided the scripts, he'd love to be a 1940s network newscaster. He even came up with a fictitious name, Ed Baxter. If anyone were to ask, Ed was the father (since we were living in the 1940s) of Ted Baxter, who was a television newscaster on the 1970s situation-comedy TV show "The Mary Tyler Moore Show."

I got busy researching and writing and "Ed" recorded, and before long, we were able to air a report each day. Over the next few years, as I found more and better sources of information, we produced enhanced versions of the newscasts, many including the actual voices of the newsmakers.

I cannot take full credit for the greatness which the 1940s/ Big Band channel would achieve as we progressed through the first decade of the 21st century. To my benefit and the benefit of all who would become listeners to the Savoy Express, one day about the time we were preparing to launch the XM Radio service, one of the world's leading musicologists, when it comes to popular recorded music spanning the period from its early days in the 1920s through the 1970s, appeared at my desk. His name was Bob Moke. Not only did Bob know the

Bob Moke

music, he had the original 78-rpm recordings, as well as many reissues on LPs, 45s, and CDs.

This was immediately fortuitous; Bob was able and willing to begin providing the many musical selections needed to fill out our library, as many of the great songs from our era had not yet been released on CD. As I made a list, Bob would go into his vault and pull out the recording, run it through a computer restoration process, and transfer it to a CD for us to load into our XM system. This arrangement continued for more than two years, until, finally, XM management allowed his joining the staff on a part-time basis.

In this same vein, in late 2002 I made a discovery that, to my mind would become a hallmark moment in my radio career—an entity named Radio Archives had just released a set of CDs containing a digital restoration of NBC Radio's broadcast coverage of the first forty hours of the D-Day invasion, which the National Broadcasting Company had preserved through reference transcriptions. Remember, this was prior to the era of tape recording. I had another "light bulb" moment: what if I could pull the key reports and announcements from these discs, and then create scripting to introduce them and clearly tell the listeners what was happening and set a time line, such as, "The time is 9:00 a.m. Eastern War Time, June 6, 1944. You are on board the Savoy Express, rolling down XM Track Number Four. Now to London for a report from NBC newsman David Anderson..." and insert them within the regular musical programming?

Along with managing the channel, preparing new daily newscasts, and also handling a second channel which I'd taken on—which I'll discuss in a moment—it took a good year to create this two-day-long audio special. First, I needed to review the entire forty-two hours of recordings, and then time and extract the appropriate NBC news elements, followed by scripting the wrap-arounds of those segments plus the intervening announcements which identified it all as special coverage of the massive landing of Allied forces on the Normandy coast of France. There were no complaints on my part; even though I had brought this extra work on myself, the adrenaline was flowing! We were creating something unique for our audience, unlike what anyone else would produce.

Before we go further, let me share a little about what quickly became known as the D-Day invasion... the largest amphibious military operation in history. By land, sea and air... taking part were 6,000 naval ships and landing craft... 12,000 aircraft...130,000 Allied troops, 18,000 of them parachuting behind enemy lines... invading Hitler's Europe!

Beginning at 12:41 a.m. EWT (Eastern War Time, equivalent to Daylight Saving Time), June 6, 1944, the Savoy Express would be in full coverage mode of this Allied landing, opening of a "western front" in the battle to free the European continent from the Nazi clutches. (Here in early June 1944, it was truly the beginning of the final phase of the war in Europe, as Allied troops in Italy had freed Rome from Nazi occupation less than twenty-four hours earlier.)

Our special D-Day coverage would continue through 5:45 p.m. EWT on June 7th... thanks to "the resources of the National Broadcasting Company"–a total of forty-one hours. More than ten hours of this time featured the original NBC 1944 audio, making the entire presentation authentic, as listeners heard the voices of many of the prominent newscasters and commentators of the era, names like H. V. Kaltenborn, Morgan Beatty, and Richard Harkness.

While the CD set provided everything we needed, there were some errors in sequencing and timings. My goal was to air the special on June 6 and 7 of 2004, exactly sixty years after the original broadcast, and to air it as an accurate minute-by-minute presentation. I discovered that in the Library of Congress sat the original second-by-second documentation of what had been sent out on the NBC radio network, as typed by a clerk at the time of broadcast; all I had to do was go over there and photocopy the pages.

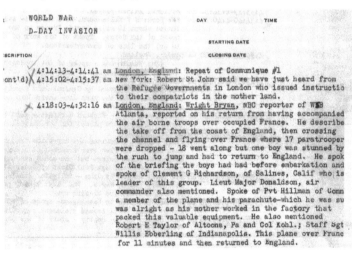

The original NBC radio broadcast log from June 6, 1944

With scripts in hand, both "Ed" and George Taylor Morris, who had been the channel's imaging voices from its earliest days, went into the studio and recorded their voice tracks. Then, all that remained was to assemble all the elements into a finished presentation, following the NBC documentation for timing and making sure that all music included had been released prior to June 1944.

George, who was also known as "GTM," had spent many years in contemporary music radio before coming to XM, serving at various times as a music host, newscaster, and/or interviewer, primarily in the greater New York area. With a kind and gentle personality, he was always ready to help. George was taken from us by cancer much too early, in 2009; he is still greatly missed.

George Taylor Morris

As I noted was the case for us in Thule, Greenland... all of the news reports coming from Europe during World War II came via shortwave radio. (Yes, there was the undersea telephone cable connecting the U.S. with England but, obviously, this was reserved for military use, and satellites were still decades away.) And as was still the case fifteen years later, shortwave transmission was unreliable and inconsistent, continually impacted by atmospheric conditions and even the time of day. The engineers had to change frequencies often to gain clarity and reduce the static. The engineer handling the receiver in New York needed to be extremely careful in his tuning as well, as it was easy to latch onto someone else's transmission without realizing it––as was evident on at least a couple of occasions during this forty-hour period, when someone else's report would end up on NBC's air.

In addition to our daily newscasts and the D-Day special coverage, we'd present edited versions of several of President

Franklin D. Roosevelt's many "fireside chats" on the month and day of which they were originally broadcast.

Meanwhile, in the middle of 2002... it was announced that although Easy Listening was not part of the original XM channel lineup, subscriber demand was such that an Easy Listening channel was to be included with three other genres when the channel lineup was realigned in August of 2002, carrying the name of SUNNY.

I quickly discovered that Lee Abrams and the rest of management really didn't recognize what kind of musical sound was being asked for, so it was time for me to become an advocate for what the subscribers really wanted; considering that the "father of the format" was already on staff, they had no choice but to place the channel under my auspices.

It wasn't that I really needed something more to do. However, I was confidently able to tell them that if they began airing the format they had in mind, to be provided by an outside source I'll discuss in a moment, the company would be losing two ways: (1) we'd not be delivering the product being requested, and (2) valuable bandwidth (which was already in scarce supply) would be eaten up by a format which wasn't necessarily desired.

That outside source was the terrestrial station operator Clear Channel Broadcasting (now known as iHeart Media), who had bought into the company when it needed funds for construction and, as part of the deal, got ownership of several channels to program as they chose. XM management's idea—since it was a format they had little personal interest in—was to let Clear Channel handle it. And that's how the channel got the SUNNY name; it was a format name they owned and wanted used.

Once I got the go-ahead, we had barely a month to assemble the musical library and structure the format. Fortunately, from decades of experience, I knew exactly what to play and that the greatest percentage of the recordings sat on CDs in my basement, so the task was not daunting. It was an immediate hit, and when subscriber listening was surveyed a few months later, SUNNY was among the dozen most-listened-to channels. Its popularity continues without waning to this day.

It was a rather momentous time for me... SUNNY launched on August 26, 2002. Just two days prior, we hosted a very special event on the 40s Channel... the first of two live broadcasts from our XM Performance Theater by the present-day Glenn Miller Orchestra, as led by Larry O'Brien.

Trombonist–as was Glenn himself–and leader of the Glenn Miller Orchestra, Larry O'Brien, during a live broadcast from the XM Performance Theater in 2002.

Both broadcasts, which took place two years apart, were recorded and are still available today through the Orchestra's website.

When we were finally able to have Bob Moke come on board in January 2004 at least part-time, it took a lot of pressure off of me. The year 2003 had been consumed by researching and writing the daily news reports and designing and scripting the D-Day special along with maintaining the daily schedules plus adding music to the libraries of both the Savoy Express and SUNNY.

Bob's arrival allowed me to devote more time to finalizing the forty-one hours of the D-Day special, which we aired beginning with the first bulletin broadcast by NBC at 12:41 a.m.

Eastern War Time (equivalent to Daylight Savings Time) on June 6, exactly sixty years to the minute after it was originally heard. We would repeat the presentation again in 2007, with lesser productions on two other occasions, using coverage aired by the Columbia Broadcasting System.

When Bob was upgraded to a full-time position in early 2006, he took on even greater responsibility for the Savoy Express and expanding and enhancing its musical library; it reached a point where I felt confident in calling it the greatest aural documentation of the World War II and Big Band era to be found anywhere in the world, both musically and historically.

At this time, he began producing weekly features such as a top hits countdown for the particular week in some year between 1936 and 1949, much in the way we were handling the newscasts, and added a feature called the Record Museum, which played songs from the 1920s and early- to mid-1930s. During Academy Awards season, Bob Moke regularly introduced and played all of the Academy Award-nominated songs for a particular year between 1936 and 1949. In an effort to keep his name alive, the family of Bing Crosby had the transcriptions of his Philco Radio Time and Kraft Music Hall network radio shows restored and transferred to CD. We were then invited to air them, and they became a twice-weekly "stop" on the Savoy Express schedule.

From day one, the company's marketing approach was to only promote the entire spectrum of programming being offered on the 100 or more channels available—although as technology progressed, it became possible to add more and more channels.

As you likely know, the major portion of satellite radio's

revenue comes from subscription fees. Fairly early on, I began to feel opportunities were being missed by using only this "buckshot" approach. I began proposing to XM management that subscriber growth could be enhanced by targeting the older segment of the nation's population, as we offered a great source of entertainment with significant appeal to them, not available anywhere else.

I recommended the purchase of a full-page ad in each issue of the *AARP Bulletin*, a tabloid newspaper published several times a year. The ads would promote only four of our channels, each of which would be highly attractive to a part of this group. Those four channels were/are SUNNY/Escape, 1940s Channel/Savoy Express, the Sinatra Channel, and Radio Classics, which features the shows from the heyday of radio. Of course, no action was ever taken on the idea—too logical, I presume. Today, this "all-channel" approach is still the singular way the merged SiriusXM markets and advertises its service.

In the early fall of 2004, it was announced that XM would launch an online service on November 15, whereby the sixty-nine XM music channels would be available for listening via our Internet site. In addition, four new music genres were to be offered but would be available online only. One of those was to be a Southern Gospel music format, which I'd later be told had been one of the five most-asked-for musical genres since XM Radio had begun three years earlier.

Management did not ask me to be involved; however, they did assign the task to "Country Dan" Dixon, who was a much-loved DJ on our *America* channel and who happened to present a one-hour country Gospel program on Sunday mornings. Since management had little interest in the genre, they were not going to provide the channel with its own program director. Dan was instructed to "throw something together we can call Southern Gospel." As Dan already had a full plate of work, and since he had little experience in structuring a format within our digital scheduling system, he came to me for help.

Always ready for a new challenge, what was I to do but jump in and help? While I had an affinity for the music, I had not really listened to it to any great extent and was not familiar with the artists. First of all, what artists and songs did we need to be playing? In researching, I discovered the genre's principal print publication was *Singing News*. I called their offices in Boone, North Carolina, and had them overnight us their last six issues— we needed a quick education if we were to construct a format that would have a chance of success. After garnering key music information, we did a search of the tens of thousands of tracks that had been loaded into our giant digital music tub. It was the same situation as we had had with SUNNY: there was little of this genre to be found.

In this case, I called the promotions person at three different Southern Gospel record companies and told them our story. Each quickly sent us a box of thirty CDs, and we were off and running! It so happened that in late October, Bill and Gloria Gaither's very popular *Gaither Homecoming Tour* was coming to an arena in Northern Virginia; very convenient to our base at XM Radio headquarters in the nation's capital. Securing passes to hang out in the Green Room gave us the opportunity to meet any number of the genre's leading artists, with the family group the Isaacs even recording an impromptu channel jingle for us, which was heard regularly on the channel for many years. Timing was with us as, up to that very day, the channel had yet to have a name. Finding a workable name that was not already trademarked was a challenge, but management had finally settled on enLighten.

With Bob Moke watching over the 40s/Savoy Express and with SUNNY in pretty good shape musically, I was comfortable devoting my primary energies to getting enLighten rolling. I won't claim that we were great, or even close to it when the channel launched on November 15, yet we were delivering pure Southern Gospel music around the clock. I can't say that I had great confidence that we'd pick up any amount of listenership as, at the time, there were two or three other sources of nonstop Southern Gospel on the web. With most of the voices that'd

be heard on the channel being male, I wanted a female voice to deliver the identifying liners. Since most of the female voices at XM were being heard on channels whose programming might not fit well with the values of those who'd be listening to enLighten, I decided to avoid them and utilize my wife Alicia, and she continued to be that voice for nearly a decade.

My beloved companion, housemate, and wife of 42 years. (Courtesy of CM Photos)

Over the following months, we continued to search out the best recordings of the prime groups and soloists, both those who were currently popular and those who were tops in previous decades, such as the Cathedrals and the Goodmans. While some critics took issue with my decision, I chose to give some exposure to recordings by lesser-known groups and soloists when I felt their singing was up to par and the song's message was inspiring.

As time passed, we began to receive a small amount of email, mostly simply saying "thank you" or asking about a particular recording. We were nearing the end of our first year when it was announced that XM's music channels would become the music service offered by DirecTV and that enLighten was to be included. This said to me that the channel had been receiving enough tune-ins that management felt it had a future. Not long after it became available on DirecTV, our listener email had more than quadrupled.

enLighten logo – © SiriusXM

By this time, we had a new Executive Vice-President of Programming, Erik Logan, who recognized that Southern Gospel—which I describe as a "cousin" of barbershop singing, as both are based on four-part harmony—was more than simply a niche genre and its fans were more than a minor portion of the population living only in the Deep South. With this recognition by management, it wasn't far into 2006 before I was told that enLighten would be joining the satellite lineup when the next channel realignment took place, which occurred on Easter Sunday night, April 16.

During the years when XM Radio was a separate company, an outside research firm would survey subscribers as to what they were listening to, much as ratings services do and have done for radio and TV across the nation for decades. Within three months of being added to the satellite service, enLighten ranked within the three dozen most-listened-to channels, well ahead of several of the highly touted channels and not far behind the 40s Channel, with the Easy Listening/Beautiful Music channel well ahead. Much to my surprise, in an XM all-employee gathering early in 2007, our Southern Gospel baby was declared to be the "XM Radio programming success story of 2006!"

Unlike the 40s Channel and SUNNY, this format took me into a whole new realm: This was a current-day genre, with the majority of the artists and groups still very much alive and still recording and performing. While not too many groups came to the Washington, D.C., area, we did have a number come do a live broadcast from our XM Performance Theater. Plus, we recorded or broadcast performances from other locations, such as the National Quartet Convention, the biggest annual event in Southern Gospel. It's a week-long gathering that was held each September at the Expo Center in Louisville, Kentucky, with most everyone who was anybody in the genre in attendance. For several years, we'd broadcast live from there each evening throughout the week, presenting artist interviews plus musical performances from the main stage in Freedom Hall.

Early in 2006, Country Dan came across a young radio personality in Georgia who we heard doing an interview with a Southern Gospel artist. Dan thought it'd be great to have this gentleman produce a weekly one-hour music-and-chat show for us; thus was born "Daniel Britt & Friends," which aired weekly on enLighten for nearly eight years.

When I joined XM, I didn't want to be a "program director" or "format manager." While these titles may have been accurate, I considered them to be dry corporate titles. Instead, I wanted—especially in the listeners' minds—to be part of the fabric from which the channel was woven; hence, on the Savoy Express, when I spoke on the air––which wasn't often––I was "your old Station Master." For enLighten, where I was heard several times a day, but not always identifying myself, I became the "Chief Shepherd" which, as described in the Bible, was fairly low in stature, yet was responsible for his flock. My "flock," of course, was made up primarily of the channel's listeners.

As for SUNNY, in 2005, Clear Channel, seeing the XM subscriber totals growing, saw an opportunity to begin generating revenue from the channels they controlled by inserting commercials. Of course, with XM having as a key selling point of offering "69 commercial-free music channels"–which included SUNNY–the company had no option other than moving it to a new channel and giving it a new name, which was Escape. I find it interesting to observe how the human mind works. There were zero changes made in the musical content or structure– only the name and channel number changed–yet I received numerous emails from listeners who were convinced the programming was different on Escape and weren't happy.

When the merger of XM and our former competitor, Sirius, was consummated, the existing Sirius management team assumed control of the merged company, even though XM Radio had significantly more subscribers at the time. This did not particularly bode well, as the Sirius folks had a different approach when it came to programming; many talented XM programmers were let go in November 2008 when the operations were consolidated. Naturally, this is what occurs when two like organizations are melded into one. This meant that a fair amount of innovation and creativity in programming that Lee Abrams had fostered at XM disappeared as the more simplistic Sirius approach became the rule.

Sensibly, considering their obvious popularity with subscribers, as the channel lineups were merged, all three of my channels were retained and began airing on the Sirius system as well. However, I did say "goodbye" to the Savoy Express, at least as far as direct involvement was concerned. The new SiriusXM management placed it under the full supervision of Bob Moke, which made sense, as he was handling the bulk of the running of the channel anyway, and I had plenty to do with the other two channels. (Sadly, only a matter of months would pass before Bob chose to leave the company.)

For the next three years, everything rolled along quite smoothly. However, as I intimated earlier, senior management had no real love for any of these three channels that I had created, and really desired to have the bandwidth available to air programming more to their liking. You see, the government had given each company only so much space in the radio frequency spectrum, which meant that in order to add a new channel, one had to be done away with.

The first of the three to come under attack was enLighten, which management planned to downgrade to an online channel as of May 4, 2011. Even before I had been told of the plans, a devoted listener in Kentucky who was a Dish TV subscriber (Dish TV had carried the Sirius music channels as part of their service) had received a revised channel listing which would take effect in May and had observed that enLighten was no longer listed. She immediately went into action—which I did not learn about until much later—starting a "Save enLighten" Facebook page and contacting many of the major Southern Gospel groups, all of whom had e-mail contact lists totaling in the thousands.

For both the artists and the lovers of this music, enLighten had become a major source for hearing it, as in the years leading into its arrival on satellite radio, many radio stations which featured the genre had changed ownership and changed to a different format. I once had a person who'd been involved in the Southern Gospel music industry for forty years proclaim to me that enLighten was "the best thing that had happened to the genre in all those years!"

I'm told that as the day of demise approached, Customer Care and the corporate offices had already received thousands of telephone calls, e-mails, and letters, many of them cancelling their radio subscriptions. By the afternoon of May 4, CEO Mel Karmazin realized that this ill-conceived action was about to take the company off a cliff and called for a reversal. Unfortunately, from a technical standpoint, the channel change was locked in place. What could be done? A channel was being reserved for short run specials, labeled Limited Engagements. It would become enLighten's home for the next eighteen months before it was moved to a new permanent channel adjacent once again to the other two Christian music channels.

Over the previous few years, I had repeatedly requested that we employ a part-time staffer, knowledgeable in Southern Gospel music and its artists, who possessed interviewing skills and was based at our Nashville studios, as more and more of the artists were moving to Nashville or regularly visited there for recording sessions. My goal was for us to become more artist-centric by producing and airing more special programming, including concerts. Management never saw fit to facilitate this.

As I had previously moved from full-time to part-time, and not being given help with enLighten, by the summer of 2013 I felt that it was time to give up one of the two channels. While I loved working in the Southern Gospel realm, it was too hard for me to give up Escape, the format which constituted my heritage within the broadcast industry. At the end of the National Quartet Convention in September of that year, I would say "goodbye" to our legion of faithful listeners, many of whom knew me as the Chief Shepherd, as my voice had been heard on the channel on a regular, even though limited, basis.

As had been my wish for a long time, enLighten would now be based in Nashville, as Kyle Cantrell—who was already a long-time member of the SiriusXM programming family—was appointed to take over the channel's management. While Kyle has done some restructuring, I feel very positive about the changes, and with the SiriusXM studios being located in the heart of Nashville, enLighten has taken on the increased artist focus which I had long desired.

Now, my responsibilities were down to one channel, one that, honestly, had not gotten enough attention over the years. So, I delved into seeing what its primary needs were. The size of the library was not an issue, as we had nearly 5,000 individual selections in regular play, and we had not received complaints of repetition from our faithful listeners, a fair number of whom listened from early morning 'til night. Then the question arose: are there titles that we played in the days when we provided our musical programming to stations across the land which are still relevant today but are missing from our Escape library? Yes!

Working with data I had retained over the decades, I was able to ferret out quite a list; there were at least a couple of hundred titles we weren't playing, partly because I did not have them.

Thankfully, as I was able to benefit from a decade earlier by connecting with Bob Moke for the 40s/Savoy Express, for Escape I was able to contact a gentleman named Forrest Patten, who had a vast collection of recordings in the Beautiful Music/Easy Listening genre, many of which have never been reissued on CD. However, Forrest has the ability to transfer recordings from LP to CD and had already digitized many tunes we were looking for, becoming another great source for material to enhance the product we provided our devoted listeners.

As is the case with many satellite channels and regular stations that do not have live announcers on duty to identify the music and provide other information, recorded "imaging liners" are utilized, which you likely are familiar with and have heard. Somewhere along the way, reacting to a sign I saw in a local restaurant promoting its regular Thursday special feature, I came up with a new identifier slogan for the channel: "Comfort Food for the Ears!" Based on references that began showing up in e-mails from listeners, it was resonating with the audience better than any other phrase or slogan we ever tried. In fact, it's the only one I can think of that ever was fed back to us.

While I was no longer involved, the 40s Channel—the first of the three that I had birthed for the company—was the next to come under attack. Beginning on March 26, 2014, it was pre-empted for three months in order to air a "limited engagement" presentation focused on Billy Joel, his life, and music. The listeners had been told it was only for this short period, but many of them did not react well to losing their favorite channel, either cancelling their subscription or demanding a refund. However, you can be certain that, if the outcry had not been so great, "the 1940s and a whole lot more" would never have returned to satellite radio! Again, the management of this company, who supposedly values its thirty million subscribers, got the message and brought the channel back at the end of the ninety-day period— and did so with a fair amount of fanfare.

As I've previously observed, all three channels have had a solid following and contribute significantly to the subscriber numbers, and have since their earliest days, with Escape being the most listened to of the three channels. This research also showed that the greatest percentage of subscribers to satellite radio typically listen to no more than three different channels, if that many, even though the Company touts its 200 or so total channels. On this subject, some of the devoted 40s listeners also listen to the Sinatra Channel, and others will go to a channel currently airing a baseball game when their favorite team is playing. I also found that if an enLighten listener takes a break, he or she more than likely goes to Escape.

With the arrival of 2015, I knew it would soon be time to make a decision; I had a monumental birthday rapidly approaching, and I had brought Escape up to the level of content and quality where I felt there wasn't much else I could do to improve it, so managing it was becoming routine and the boredom factor was rearing its head. Was this the year to retire from the company? Well, come June, I had my answer. I was confidentially told that senior management had made the decision to totally eliminate the Escape channel from all platforms, with the change occurring sometime in mid-August, so my services would likely no longer be needed. I chose the end of August as my departure time, as it coincided with my birthday.

At the same time, I needed to be an advocate for the huge body of subscribers about to be disenfranchised. I did not really expect a positive response, as nothing I said was going to change their minds. However, I could not sit idly by and not make my case. As I had done for enLighten four years earlier, based on my experience and intimate understanding of the channel's listenership, I presented the facts to senior management as I saw them:

In the interest of the Company and several hundred thousand subscribers who will have no option but to cancel their subscriptions if Escape is deleted... I beg you to re-consider your proposed action.

- As is the case with the 40s Channel, the music on Escape may be from another era, but it's still the music of choice for hundreds of thousands of people in North America. And there is no other decent source for hearing it; that's why they subscribe to SiriusXM. (Plus, our collection of recordings is unequaled!) And since the heart of this format is the 1960s, the majority of those listening are still fully alive and on the road, not preparing for a nursing home. It's truly, as we call it, the "Melodies of Your Life!"
- While the music of the 1940s and 1930s lives on with a great following, I can virtually guarantee that the same exists for the music of Escape, and that the

Escape audience is larger!

- Not even planning to keep Escape alive and available online and via the app seems to be an even greater error.
- This may not be among your favorite styles of music. And, yes, it is music from another era. Yet, these are the melodies that are loved by several hundred thousand of our paying customers, being played in the primarily instrumental arrangements they love.

The one and only acknowledgement that resulted from this memo was the decision to retain it as an online channel, as was done for the Folk and Pops channels, both of which had earlier lost their satellite berths. Obviously, these were illogical actions as well; unfortunately, their fans were not able to muster sufficient forces to cause management to back-track. Based on this action and my plans to retire at the end of August, I devoted my final weeks with the company to putting the house in order, so that the channel could pretty much be run by a robot except for the holidays that we celebrated throughout the year.

When it was announced at the end of July that the channel would leave the satellite service on August 12, the clamor began; there was nothing for me to do but remain above the fray and direct listeners to Customer Care. I continued to fulfill my obligations to the company through the end of August and, two days after my 80th birthday, departed the premises for the last time.

That, my dear reader, was to be the end of my story, but this proved to not quite be the end, as I had no knowledge of what lie ahead, and that which I had predicted in June was obviously on target!

Just two weeks later, exactly a month after Escape was removed from the satellite service (on September 11), an e-mail went out to everyone who had either cancelled their radio subscriptions or called Customer Care to complain, with this message:

Beautiful Music Channel 69 returns

THE LISTENERS HAVE SPOKEN, AND IT'S COMING BACK!

We're bringing Escape back to SiriusXM. Many listeners like you let us know your passion for Escape when we removed it from the channel lineup.

We got the message: there is no substitute for the instrumental melodies on Escape. Your enthusiasm is amazing to hear, and it made our decision to bring back Escape on Channel 69 an easy one.

You will be able to find it right back on Channel 69 starting Tuesday September 15th on XM radios and in October for Sirius Radios.

When a former subscriber forwarded the announcement to me, I did not gloat. The joy that I felt in reading it was for the tens of thousands who would have their beloved music once again available to them. The other thing that warms my heart is that I now have an unblemished record, having the honor of creating three different musical formats which continue to live on, in spite of each being targeted for destruction! It proves that when a corporation is hit in the one place that hurts—their pocketbook—it's possible to have dumb decisions reversed.

I am pleased to say that throughout my nearly fifteen years with the company, under both the original XM Radio management and the totally different senior management of the merged SiriusXM, I could never allow myself to just do the job expected or specified; it was always about what more could be provided to the listeners to enhance their listening experience.

During the XM years, we were challenged to go the extra mile and were rewarded with yearly bonuses and stock option grants. Since the merger, most employees have had their required duties increased, but they have not seen increases in compensation, and the bonuses and stock options have been replaced by free pretzels and soda. Still, they soldier on, because their professional pride demands that they serve their "paying customer" well.

While there were negative incidents along the way, these fifteen years were a perfect way to cap off my personal involvement in the industry with which I've had a lifelong love affair. There is nothing I have loved more than using the gifts I was blessed with to create programming that has touched hearts and brought joy to so many, going back to when I played Christmas music from the roof of my parents' home to entertain our small Pennsylvania community.

Oh, yes, there is... my dear, beloved Alicia!

POSTSCRIPT

cannot wrap up this book without leaving you with a few additional thoughts, as well as a few writings by others I've gathered along the way.

While my last official day of employment in the broadcast industry was August 28, 2015, I still find myself, more than two years later, following industry happenings almost daily. Do I miss my involvement? Yes. However, I cannot help but be proud of my legacy as has been detailed in these preceding pages––all built on the premise of bringing joy to and making a difference in peoples' lives... doing so one by one, yet totaling millions over a 50+ year period.

Since a great percentage of my broadcast career has been tied to the Good Music/Easy Listening/Beautiful Music format, there's one more fact related to it I need to share: It's disappearance from radio in the late 1980s/early 1990s was not precipitated by listeners abandoning this style of programming... many of our stations continued to retain their large audiences. The blame can be laid at the feet of the advertising agency community, where it was declared that people fifty and older were too set in their ways... no longer capable of being swayed to try something new or different. Hence, any portion of a station's listenership which was in the upper demographic categories was discounted, meaning that these stations did not receive advertising dollars to which they were otherwise entitled. This is what led so many of our stations to switch to formats appealing to younger listeners.

This format's continued appeal is evidenced by what was described at the end of the last chapter. In 2015, nearly a quarter-of-a-century after FM stations in city after city were dropping this so-called "elevator" music format because they couldn't sell it to advertisers, when the Escape channel which aired this programming was dropped by SiriusXM, radio subscriptions were cancelled in such great numbers that management quickly reversed course and restored it. It's also been reported that this genre of music's channel on Music Choice, provider of the lineup of music channels available on many cable TV systems across the nation, is one of its most popular.

As of this writing, basic radio (AM & FM, or terrestrial radio, as we called it in satellite radio) continues to be headed in an unhealthy direction. This downward spiral had its beginnings in the mid-1990s—when the government was convinced to raise the limits on the number of radio stations that an individual or company could own in any one market, and remove all restrictions on the total they could control nationwide. Opening the floodgates, this was quickly followed by consolidation... where "big money" stepped in and started buying up stations to utilize economies of scale to reduce costs and increase profits.

These investors, who have managed to gobble up a great percentage of the best stations in most cities/markets of any size, have buried themselves in such great amounts of debt in making these acquisitions that a lot of their revenue is consumed right off just to pay the interest due.

From the very beginning, the most targeted area for savings was programming... as it takes people to deliver a quality product; yet, many in the position of making such financial decisions have no understanding of what's embodied in creating a product which attracts and connects with a person on the receiving end of a radio station, better known as "the listener." The only goal is to do it cheaper and with fewer bodies. "Wow, look at the dollars we can save!"

With programming and promotional staffs being cut to the bone––and in many smaller-market stations becoming virtually

Out-Innovate plaque

non-existent—those who were still employed were more over-worked that ever. The result is less and less "live" and "local"... and radio being further short-changed and impacted negatively due to the lack of opportunities in the areas of innovation.

On my desk sits this plaque given to me by Bonneville International Corporation's president and my boss, Mr. Arch L. Madsen. He presented it to me in 1970 after I became his hero for taking WRFM out of the dumpster and to the top with little visible advertising–after none of my several predecessors were able to move it one inch up the ladder. As you've read, the station's initial success came from our massive dial card placement effort, which generated huge word-of-mouth publicity... the kind of endorsement advertising that'd be nearly impossible to acquire through any other means. "It's amazing what you did with so few resources, begging the question... why are cash strapped groups not being more creative when it comes to marketing," was a comment made to me recently by longtime radio program director and media consultant Jerry Del Colliano—who recently was also inducted into the Philadelphia Broadcast Pioneers Hall of Fame. In the short two years that I was at the helm of WRFM, we did so many creative and innovative things and had so much fun doing them, I consider that time the greatest of my life and my career in radio broadcasting.

Yours truly with Jerry Del Colliano following his induction into the Broadcast Pioneers of Philadelphia Hall of Fame in 2016.
Photo by Leigh Richards

Jerry knows the answer to his own question, as he's written about it many times. It is not due to a lack of creative minds already in the industry, nor to a lack of young creative individuals who'd love to have an opportunity to show what they can do in radio—it's the short-sightedness of those at the top who have cut everything to the bone. This is just the opposite of what should be happening if the industry is to have a future.

While many innovative actions, as noted, can be effective without requiring big dollars, they do require a mindset involving commitment and a willingness to devote time and energy toward carrying out the plan—which is difficult when there's little staff left beyond what's needed to simply keep the station on the air. Plus, as I noted earlier, a number of the promotional things we did at WRFM, many managers would consider just too much work. In the Appendix is a reprint of an article I wrote nearly twenty years ago on the subject of innovation, which was published in *Radio World*.

Along the same line, but at a personal level... without question, so much of success in life, including getting a foothold in radio or other media, is, to quote Angela Duckworth, about "passion and perseverance"! Or, to borrow the title of Duckworth's 2016 book, it could be described simply as "grit." Popular writer Malcolm Gladwell, author of such books as *David and Goliath*, when asked during an interview, pinpointed the prime factors for success as being "the desire to win and the passion for what you're doing." He did not include such items as "skills" or "innate abilities," although they can and will certainly be contributing elements in enabling your drive for success.

As I have noted earlier, I was blessed—or you can say "gifted"—with an innate ability and intuitive sense when it came to music and creating successful radio programming. I did not learn it in any school or borrow these talents from anyone or any other source. Yet, without the motivation to seek opportunities and use these gifts, which have been displayed multiple times in this book, they would have been of little value—not one of the major advancements in my career within the broadcast industry came about by someone coming to look for Marlin and offer me a position!

When your heart is set on accomplishing whatever it is you desire, you must accept the pressure involved, and when the chips are down, keep pushing onward. After all, if you are not passionate about this, why bother? During my years with SiriusXM, I made numerous proposals and requests. Many got no response; however, the ones that did usually came back with a "no" followed by "but, Marlin, we love your passion." These responses did not stop me from continuing to propose actions and request authorization to carry out plans that I believed in and were in the interest of the listeners—which is the only reason I wanted to do them in the first place!

If you put forth ideas that you believe are worthy of consideration or being carried out, you must be prepared to ignore the naysayers. You must believe in yourself, be an advocate for the concept you are proposing, and have the passion to inspire others to see things your way.

During my Army time, I learned that the military term for gathering vital information about the "enemy" is G2, Intelligence. In the business world, this would be defined as learning and knowing everything possible about your competition or an organization that you'd like to sell to or be employed by before any direct contact is made.

I will say that it all begins with curiosity: wanting to know the whole story, how it all works and how the pieces fit together. Both my move to Boston and our acquisition of a radio station in Spokane, Washington, were entered into through a rush of emotion, replacing common sense and good judgment... and without a complete G2 investigation!

What brings this about? I have never been particularly happy with the status quo. When things would begin to get too routine or somewhat boring, with an activity or function moving into what I've seen described as "maintenance mode," I'd get itchy and begin looking for new turf to conquer, or at least attempt to. I'm more of a builder rather than simply being happy maintaining a station or format that didn't offer opportunities for creating special features or elements or the challenge of taking the product to a new level.

In the world today, moving quickly is a priority. However, it's not to be done without care. You must think through an action, which I failed to properly do in either case. However, procrastination can be a major liability as well. The key is to keep moving forward, always looking down the road to see what possible opportunities may be awaiting, and potential pitfalls as well, preparing for what action that can speed up or improve your trip.

President Theodore Roosevelt is quoted as saying, "Keep your eyes on the stars... and your feet on the ground!" During the latter part of the 20th century, nationally known radio disc jockey and show host Casey Kasem began using an updated version in his sign-off of each broadcast, "Keep your feet on the ground, and keep reaching for the stars!" I achieved all that I have in my eighty-plus years through following this approach to life.

Over a recent four-year period, PBS Television's *Masterpiece* program presented a series which was based on the life of Harry Selfridge, an American who moved to England in the early 1900s and built one of the most successful department stores—one bearing his name—in retailing history. Not only was he an acclaimed marketer and promoter, he was an outstanding leader. Take a few minutes to read and digest how these quotations attributed to Harry Selfridge can positively impact the functioning of any organization:

- People will sit up and take notice of you if you will sit up and take notice of what makes them sit up and take notice.
- The boss drives his men; the leader coaches them.
- The boss depends upon authority, the leader on goodwill.
- The boss inspires fear; the leader inspires enthusiasm.
- The boss says, "I"; the leader, "we."
- The boss fixes the blame for the breakdown; the leader fixes the breakdown.
- The boss knows how it is done; the leader shows how.
- The boss says, "Go"; the leader says, "Let's go!"

The world-renowned and celebrated humanitarian Mother

Teresa captured the meaning of leadership eloquently in this statement printed on a wall of her home for children in Calcutta, India:

- "People are often unreasonable, irrational, and self-centered. Forgive them anyway.
- If you are kind, people may accuse you of selfish, ulterior motives. Be kind anyway.
- If you are successful, you will win some unfaithful friends and some genuine enemies. Succeed anyway.
- If you are honest and sincere people may deceive you. Be honest and sincere anyway.
- What you spend years creating, others could destroy overnight. Create anyway.
- If you find serenity and happiness, some may be jealous. Be happy anyway.
- The good you do today, will often be forgotten. Do good anyway.
- Give the best you have, and it will never be enough. Give your best anyway."

I love to remind young people that they should never consider themselves to be too big or too important to take on any task. I recently read a new biography of John D. Rockefeller, who recognized early on the potential uses for oil and was the founder of Standard Oil (today known as Exxon Mobil). What may not be known about Mr. Rockefeller is that he spent a great deal of his time out with his workers, joining them at doing menial jobs in his refineries and other operations, looking at how to streamline functions and not overlook opportunities for savings. These were not meant to be ways to cut his workforce or pay his workers less (he paid his workers well, understanding how to get the best out of them); rather, he was seeking to cut costs in other ways as his business constantly faced growing competition from many quarters. He is quoted as saying, "The secret to success is to do the common things uncommonly well."

I've been honored twice in my career, in both cases by an organization devoted to preservation. The first was in 2001, by the broadcast industry's Broadcasters Foundation, whose commitment is to assisting present and former members of the industry who have fallen on hard times financially. They presented me with their American Broadcast Pioneer Award.

Yours truly being presented with the 2001 American Broadcast Pioneer Award by Broadcasters' Foundation Chairman Ed McLaughlin.

The second came in 2015, when the Broadcast Pioneers of Philadelphia inducted me into the Broadcast Pioneers Hall of Fame. Why Philadelphia? This comes from the fact that my climb up the ladder of success and recognition in this field of endeavor which has been the love of my life had its beginnings in the City of Brotherly Love in 1963. There is likely no organization doing a better job of preserving the history of broadcasting, both radio and TV, especially on a local/regional level, than the Broadcast Pioneers of Philadelphia. Its program of gathering historical documentation via print and audio and video recordings and digitizing the whole lot is a major on-going commitment.

While it was not an award as such, I felt humbly honored when the June 21, 1971, issue of *Broadcasting* magazine published a major report on the state of radio which included a photo of yours truly under which the caption read: "*Marlin knows.*" *That's the tribute a colleague pays to Marlin Taylor, general manager of WRFM (FM) New York and perhaps the leading program force in the area of "pretty music" radio—or conservative popular, as he describes it.* To this day I have no idea who that person was or might have been.

Honoring my induction into the Broadcast Pioneers of Philadelphia Hall of Fame in 2015.

I've had friends ask what is to be my next big endeavor. I can't say I really have any beyond completing this book. My main interests at this point in my life lie in preservation: preserving the great and dramatic histories of radio (to which

I hope this book might contribute a little) and railroading, and what these two industries have contributed to life in this nation. I don't see myself re-entering the radio field, and I don't believe that I have any brilliant ideas appropriate for these times. I believe I could be an asset to a radio company, but it would have to be a situation where I could "emotionally involve" myself—which was the case with most everything throughout my life—and where my counsel would be actively considered and utilized.

The final question must be—as I enter my 83rd year and look back... do I have any regrets? As I've perhaps alluded to, are there situations where I should have stood my ground, fought harder, and stayed the course? Or, are there situations or events where I could have made a greater contribution, done a better job, or been of greater service and made a difference? If I think hard, there must be a few. Related to this, I must acknowledge that somewhere along the line, I realized I have a personality trait that may not have always been helpful—if a situation looks hopeless or I've simply "had it up to here," my favored action is to cut and move on.

Somewhere along the way I scribbled down two philosophical thoughts. The first is, "Think higher and feel deeper," from author & Nobel Laureate Elie Weisel. The second is, "Indifference is worse than hatred," not attributed to any one person (in researching, I found several variations).

After wrapping up 60+ years in the working/business world, primarily in broadcasting, I leave you with these bits of counsel:

- Step up! Take a risk! Be proactive!
- Live the "more" approach: do more, give more, and give your best, always!
- Commit to learn something new every day, no matter how small it may be.
- Never think or say, "That's not my job!"

And finally, for anyone working in the field of mass communications, the first and foremost rule must be recognizing and delivering what's in the best interests and tastes of the listener/viewer/reader, as that is the reason for a radio or television station or publication to exist and the number one priority for achieving success!

APPENDIX

On the following pages, you'll find four commentaries written by yours truly in the latter part of the last century, making them truly "historical" documents at this point, as so much in the radio industry has changed. Hence, while what I've written and propose may well make sense, when considering today's conditions and "atmosphere," there's little likelihood an owner or manager will give them consideration.

WHO'S TENDING THE STORE, OR WHO'S LEADING THE PARADE, OR HOW'S YOUR MIRROR IMAGE?

Like many others who have written in these pages, I have pondered the question: Why are there so many failing radio stations in this country? Is that the way it's meant to be? What other industry—except possibly the steel industry—has such a high percentage of the total that are not making it?

I have trouble accepting this, because I feel there's no justifiable reason. I love the radio business and it's my belief that any radio station with enough of a signal to reach warm bodies can be a winner. Maybe not in the Arbitron, but to the extent that it delivers a meaningful product, serves a purpose, and can develop the financial wherewithal to support itself.

Running a successful station isn't easy. Yet, I don't believe it's really a lot more difficult than running an unsuccessful one. It's certainly a lot more fun being a winner.

I'm immediately suspect when I talk with a manager or owner whose station's not making it and the excuses start. You've heard them at one time or another. They tell you about the fallacies of the ratings service, the two new salespersons hired on Monday who haven't had an order yet, the night jock who keeps screwing up the music rotation and so on. I'll always remember a major market manager who's constant complaint was about how he couldn't improve his cash flow because a prime competitor was unfairly decreasing rates, Yet, his station always had significantly better ratings than the culprit in question.

Do these folks enjoy being perpetual underdogs? In most cases, no. It's more likely the Peter Principle at work. You remember Dr. Lawrence J. Peter and his very logical theory of a person being promoted to a level above his capability and comfort zone. We see it so frequently in radio. Top sales rep to sales manager. Sales manager to GM. DJ to PD. My personal observation over the years has been that the better the performer, whether is air work or sales, the poorer his performance will be in a management role. And, when a person is out of his or her element, they run scared.

J. P. Morgan, the rich banker who died before most of us were born, once said, "Only an optimist can win in playing the game of business." It's still very true today. You've got to visualize success before you can achieve it. If one dwells on the negative, there's no way his mind can paint pictures of large numbers in the revenue ledger or the Arbitron report or building the bridge needed to reach them.

Today, lack of success certainly can't be blamed on lack of available help. While radio is more competitive, there are programming and sales consultants, training courses, sales support materials and computerized music, traffic and billing systems. Or, read the various trade publications. Week after week, there are articles and items dealing with every aspect of successful station operation.

With all these resources at hand, why are stations still failing? The answer is simple... a lot of somebody's aren't doing their jobs. The stated reason will always place the blame on others. "The FCC wouldn't give us a power increase" or "the jocks wouldn't play the right records" or "we couldn't find people who could sell."

Stop and think about it, isn't failure a "mirror" matter? If you are a manager and you have a business that is doing poorly, where does the fault really lie? Who is the one charged with leading it to success? If staff members do not do their jobs properly or well enough to win, is it not ultimately your responsibility?

Note the word "leading" in the paragraph above. The bottom line is that we have a leadership crisis in our country and in our industry today. Where are more of those men and women with courage, with vision, with spirit and drive, willing to step forward and put their lives on the firing line in radio's battle to maintain its position on the mountaintop and conquer new territory?

As was said the other day, if the Koreans ever decide to give up their vegetable stands and move into radio, a good many in this industry will probably end up selling space in weekly newspapers. I don't believe we are short on creativity and good ideas. We're short on people willing to get off their duffs and work. We'd go broke running vegetable stands.

Originally published in *The Pulse of Broadcasting* in the latter 1980s. Reprinted by permission.

NOTE: It was about this time that we acquired the AM station in Spokane, Washington, as detailed in Chapter 12. If I had seen any increase in the potential for it reaching a self-sustaining position and we had not been running out of resources, I believe we would have stayed in the fray. Of course, today, some 25+ years later, the KRSS format... known as Contemporary Christian Music, is a major programming format in many markets across the U. S.

THE ATTITUDE FACTOR

"Where's he coming from?" This might very well be your first reaction to that headline. I've seen very little written on this subject, yet it is one of the key elements in the success formula of business as well as living in general.

The attitude of the team of people called the staff is what in many cases makes the difference between being a very successful radio station and one that's just good. If you're one of those broadcast people who spend part of their life listening to stations wherever you go, I know you've arrived in a new market, listened to several stations and done your grading and critiquing. Then you've gotten a look at the ratings report, only to be surprised to find that the station or stations you judged the best were second and third . . . or lower. An "average sounding" station, in your analysis, is leading the pack.

Is this a fluke in the survey? I doubt it. It's the "attitude factor" at work. Attitude, in case you haven't checked its definition in the dictionary lately, means "a mental position; a feeling or emotion toward..." your station, your job or simply your lot in life.

A station can have the tallest stick and most powerful signal, the biggest promotion budget, a high-priced TV spot and the best technicians when it comes to programming, promoting and engineering and still not succeed. Why? Because nobody thought to add the key ingredient. The team didn't have "soul" . . . there was no passion to win!

I like to talk about my favorite person, my redheaded wife. She's a singer. She may not be as technically perfect as some others and there may be a few sopranos around with a bigger, more beautiful voice, but there are few singers, if any, who can move an audience the way Alicia can and does. She feels every note of what she's singing and communicates the message to the listener.

Maybe I should call it the "Love Factor." Because a positive attitude amounts to loving your work and loving the place you work and loving those who listen to your station. A truly successful air person is one who turns on the mike and "makes love" to the person who's on the other end of the radio. A good actor can put one over on the audience, but most of us show our real feelings, no matter how hard we try to hide them.

While the technicians worry about more research, how many cuts to add to the re-current category and how short the newscasts should be, your station's concentration on creating the most sincere, enthusiastic, loving, caring radio station in America will place you and it on the fast track to riches. I'm not saying to ignore these other elements or that they're not important. However, without the right attitude . . . a genuine love for your work and a committed, unfailing belief––by the entire team––that you can and will win, it's not likely to happen to your station.

Originally published in *The Pulse of Broadcasting*'s May 4, 1987 issue. Reprinted by permission.

INNOVATION BEATS THE COMPETITION

To out-distance our competition, we have to out-innovate them! Is this your approach to managing and leading? If your answer is yes, I congratulate you.

A plaque containing this statement has sat on my desk for years, since achieving early ratings success at former New York station WRFM, where we used several innovative concepts to roll past two long-entrenched head-on competitors in a matter of months. It was a gift from my boss at the time, the late Arch Madsen, president of Bonneville International Corporation.

The Webster's New Collegiate Dictionary definition of "innovation" is the "introduction of something new ... a new idea or method." A secondary definition is to "apply creativity."

Ho-hum is a no-no

For a broadcaster, innovation means *seizing the moment* on a daily basis to effect an increase in listenership value to the benefit of your advertising clients.

Why are we discussing "innovation" in a progressive industry like ours? Granted, there are many creative people in radio doing a lot of innovative things. However, when you judge the industry based on its impact upon listeners, most commercial radio stations fall into a "ho-hum" category when a person tunes in. An innovative radio station should generate a "wow" reaction in a listener. It's to the "ho-hum" stations that I specifically target my comments.

If you manage one of these stations, do yourself a giant favor right now. Raise your sights, muster the courage, pop a can of spinach and address the challenge head-on!

First of all, recognize that, with few exceptions, you can do things that make your station more "listener-friendly." Also, remember that the programming you think has lots of appeal might rate much lower with listeners in your community.

Where might radio be today were it not for Gordon McLendon, one of the greatest innovators this industry has ever seen? McLendon pioneered the top 40, all-news and beautiful music formats. Paul Drew said of McLendon, "he read the public taste and where it was going better than anyone. McLendon dared to be great and he was."

McLendon would never have been successful or be remembered if he had not been an innovative thinker and, most importantly, willing to risk taking his ideas to air. He was not afraid to shake up a successful format if he believed it was time for a change.

More recently, look at what radio might have missed out on if Jeff Smulyan had not been willing to risk the big bucks required to launch the innovative concept of all-sports radio on WFAN (AM) in New York. Or Ed McLaughlin going out on a limb, believing an audience would support a daytime talk show hosted by an individual who was unknown, highly opinionated and had a definite conservative bent. Love him or not, we all know what Rush Limbaugh has done for talk radio.

Incremental innovation

Innovation should be high on the mind and heart of every management person. Most actions will not be as momentous as those mentioned earlier, nor do they need to be.

You never know if a creative change might turn out to be just as important to the future of your station. Maybe your idea will be copied across the industry. That happened with an idea we implemented at WRFM on the spur-of-the-moment.

We had restructured the format of a station and needed to generate word-of-mouth. Our goal was to take the station "from worst to second." Our promotional budget was smaller than that for office supplies, so innovation was our only option.

We had a shortage of advertisers. So, in true innovative fashion, we carved out a couple of commercial-free hours each day, creating the "Total Music Hour." We simply announced, "In the next 60 minutes, you'll hear 59 minutes of music." It gave the station a unique feature with a hook, to promote both on and off the air.

We told our audience to "be listening for the next Total Music Hour," but never announced when the next hour would come. The tactic generated great word-of-mouth for us.

Innovative thinking is not necessarily just for management. Involve the entire staff. Be open to ideas. Who's the most creative thinker on your station team?

Low-cost

What can you do that's new or different to make listeners sit up and take notice, possibly create word-of-mouth, cause the local newspaper or TV station to do a story on you or give your sales reps a new piece of ammo? That's what innovation is all about.

Innovation does not have to cost much. Just apply brain power to an existing situation or opportunity. In fact, I bet you can take action today to produce savings and create a better-sounding radio station.

Consider this: Your innovative step may not involve adding anything. Instead, it could be a return to the basics from which you strayed or removal of an irritant that serves no useful purpose.

This article appeared in the *Radio World* issue dated May 13, 1998.

EASY LISTENING: THE ROOTS OF SUCCESS

It's just 10 minutes before midnight. The engineer is soldering the last wire in the on-air studio. There's excitement in the air. The date is September 14, 1967–twenty years ago. Moments from now–at the stroke of 12–WJIB will sign on as Boston's newest radio station.

As the Music and Program Director for the station, I was on the scene along with several others, anxiously awaiting the big moment. We all knew that the Boston market was ready for what we would offer. However, we were not prepared for what was to happen in the weeks to follow. The outpouring of enthusiasm from the listening public was exciting, causing this soul to realize the magnitude to which radio can touch and warm people's hearts.

The *Boston Globe*, a minority owner of the station, was deluged with letters to the Editor, filled with glowing phrases and thank you's. A couple of suburban newspapers even printed editorials lauding WJIB's arrival. (When's the last time you saw that?)

It was no later than December when ad agencies began to call, looking for rate and avail information so orders could be placed. Wow, you say. This was not all that easy for us to handle, as we had no one on staff prepared to sell advertising. WJIB's owners, Kaiser Broadcasting, may have well been the first to consciously plan to run a station commercial-free for its first three months on air. Suddenly, we had advertising but no sales staff. It was at that time the station's present GM, Charlie Pickering, joined the staff to handle sales.

WJIB was not Boston's first "Good Music" station. (In

those days the term "Easy Listening" had not been coined, at least not applied to that format. And, we had not yet reached the 70's, when "Beautiful Music" would become the format's handle.) An AM station, WEZE, had been on the air for several years and consistently ranked in Boston's top four or five stations.

What was WEZE's downfall, causing it to lose two-thirds of its audience within six months after WJIB's arrival? In 1967 this was not yet a case of FM band dominance over AM. Part of the answer certainly relates to it being a typical full-service station of the 60's, airing two newscasts every hour and carrying a heavy commercial load. Consequently, WJIB played nearly 50% more music . . . 57 minutes versus 40 minutes per hour. I don't believe this, either, was the major deciding factor.

While both stations were properly defined as Good Music stations–in that they aired a large percentage of instrumentals– there was a great difference in content of titles. WJIB played titles from the sixties, fifties and forties. WEZE's music, for the most part, was still rooted in the twenties and thirties––with heavy emphasis on early-century composers such as Sigmund Romberg and Victor Herbert. (If you don't know who Romberg and Herbert are, ask your grandmother . . . she may remember.)

Nineteen-sixty-seven was a landmark year in Boston radio. About six months prior to WJIB's arrival, a lazy full-service "non-entity" AM station named WNAC changed its calls to WRKO and format to Bill Drake's "Top 23" and shook Beantown to it proverbial roots. Again, this was not Boston's first or only Top-40 station.

Both stations were dramatically successful because they gave the listeners what they wanted. And what better approach to success in business than serving your customer to the fullest? However, today, it's clearly evident that too many managers in Easy Listening––and in all of radio for that matter––are not listening, are not being sensitive to their listeners.

As we enter 1988, the greatest danger Easy Listening faces as a format is seeking to achieve changes in demographic make-up through indiscriminate modification of the music. Doing this can easily destroy what Easy Listening/Beautiful Music has been offering so successfully, for three decades: a unique service that provides relaxation and escape. When you take away those qualities, you take away the heart of the format...and end up with a product that truly satisfies no one.

The greatest challenge––and opportunity––in the months ahead is to better focus on the core audience. This doesn't necessarily mean no changes. And, it does not mean that the format shouldn't have energy and a contemporary flavor. It does mean letting the format's music evolve as tastes change, rather than adding recordings that, instead of becoming true "hooks" for new listeners, become irritants to existing listeners. It does mean turning one's attention, as researchers Bill Moyes and John Coleman recommend, toward doing a better job of positioning and marketing our Easy Listening stations to expand our circle of influence.

This commentary appeared in *The Pulse of Broadcasting* in late 1987.

INDEX

X

Z